IEE TELECOMMUNICATIONS SERIES 22

Series Editors: Professor J. E. Flood
Professor C. J. Hughes
Professor J. D. Parsons

Data communications and networks 2

Other volumes in this series:

Data communications and networks 2

Edited by R.L.Brewster

Peter Peregrinus Ltd. on behalf of
the Institution of Electrical Engineers

Published by: Peter Peregrinus Ltd., London, United Kingdom

© 1989: Peter Peregrinus Ltd.

British Library Cataloguing in Publication Data

Brewster, R. L. (Ronald L, 1932-)
    Data communications and networks 2.
    1. Computer systems. Networks
    I. Title   II. Institution of Electrical Engineers
    004.6
ISBN 0-86341-190-8

Printed in England by Short Run Press Ltd., Exeter

Contents

List of Contributors

Chapter 1
D.W.F. Medcraft,
Chief Engineer,
British Telecom,
London & South East.

Chapter 2
John T.L. Sharpe,
Marconi Communication Systems

Chapter 3
Dr Ron Brewster,
Department of Electrical and
    Electronic Engineering and
    Applied Physics
Aston University.

Chapter 4
J.D. Ash
GEC Plessey Telecommunications Ltd.

Chapter 5
B.G. West and P.G. Wright
Mobile Communications Group
GEC-Marconi Research Centre.

Chapter 6
Dr Ron Brewster,
Deptartment of Electrical and
    Electronic Engineering and
    Applied Physics,
Aston University.

Chapter 7
A. Clark,
British Telecom Datacomms.

Chapter 8
J. Hovell,
Research & Technology
British Telecom Research
Laboratories.

Chapter 9
Prof. Steve R. Wilbur,
University College London.

Chapter 10
Tony Gale,
Network Systems,
International Computers Ltd.

Chapter 11
P. J. Munday,
Racal Research Ltd.

Chapter 12
J. P. Chambers,
BBC Research Department.

Chapter 13
Peter Karry,
Telecoms Industry Unit,
ICL (UK) Ltd.

Preface

The requirement for data communication is closely linked to the invention and development of the digital computer. The first commercially viable computers emerged during the late 1950s and were relatively simple devices, accessed by a single terminal directly associated with the computer hardware. However, the data handling capacity of computers was soon realised and in the early 1960s an airline seat reservation scheme was introduced which required access to a central computer from terminals situated remotely from the computer mainframe. Thus data transmission was born. In the ensuing 25 years there has been an enormous growth in computing power and facilities and in data processing applications. The provision of data communication facilities has, therefore, likewise increased beyond the wildest imaginations of those of us involved with data transmission at its inception in the 1960s.

In the earliest days of data transmission, the only readily available medium with easy access to almost any location in the world was the telephone network. Although not designed to convey digital signals, its very ubiquitousness made it a prime candidate for the transmission of data. Despite its limitations, it served well as the almost exclusive carrier of data signals for a decade or more. In order to interface with the analogue environment of the telephone network, modems were designed to convert the digital signals into signals with a spectral content more like that of telephone speech signals. The first modems appeared in public service in the UK in 1965 and offered data throughput rates of 1200 bits/s half-duplex or 200 bits/s full-duplex over the switched telephone network. Since that date more sophisticated modems have been developed using complex modulation schemes and incorporating adaptive equalisation. These have extended the data rates available over the telephone network to a rate of 9600 bits/s. This seems to be an upper limit and even this requires specially selected lines.

The inadequacy of the telephone network for many data applications was soon realised and dedicated data networks were developed for specific applications. A range of local area networks (LANs) using ring and bus topologies were developed for networks confined to a factory complex or campus. Larger private 'wide area networks (WANs) were developed for national, and even international, use. Public data networks employing packet switching were introduced for specifically data communication purposes.

Alongside the development of specifically data networks, an interesting development was taking place in telephony. The transmission of telephone signals was gradually being changed from an analogue to a digital mode of transmission using pulse-code-modulation. This meant that trunk telephone transmission was now to be carried out on circuits with a digital capability based on multiples of 64 kbits/s, the basic pcm rate per telephone channel. 30 channel pcm uses a line rate of 2Mbits/s. With the introduction of digitally transmitted telephony, it became an obvious progression to introduce digital switching into the telephone network. This is now a reality and the next step is the introduction of an integrated services digital network (ISDN) which will handle all signals, telephony or data, on a single network. Present plans are for a widely available ISDN in use by the turn of the century and, unless overtaken by events, is likely to happen.

The growth in the use of large data networks and in the variety of tasks that the host computers are being asked to perform means that there is an urgent need for standardisation of network interfaces and protocols. Much has happened recently in the area of strategies for 'Open Systems Interconnection' and in the production of recommendations and specifications for interconnection standards. The purpose of this book is to survey the current state-of-the-art in data communications and networks and to indicate the direction in which the networks are likely to be developing in the future. Details of standards and interfaces have been included because, without these, no reasonable network strategy would be possible.

The book is based on notes prepared for the Institution of Electrical Engineers Vacation School on 'Data Communications and Networks' to be held at Aston University in September 1989. It supercedes the earlier edition of the book, based on the notes of the same school held in September 1985. In the four intervening years much has happened, especially with regard to the establishment of standards for ISDN and for the higher level protocols of the OSI model. The original book has enjoyed wide popularity but it now appears very dated. It is hoped that this new edition, which has been extensively rewritten, will be as popular as its predecessor.

I should like to thank the authors of the various chapers for their valuable contribution to the book, The preparation of the manuscripts has made a significant demand on the valuable time of many busy people and without their dedicated help this book would not have been possible. Thanks are also due to those unnamed, but nevertheless very important people, who have advised, typed, proof-read and helped in various ways with the production of the book.

Ron Brewster
Aston, August 1989

Chapter 1

Introduction

D.W.F.Medcraft

1.1   INTRODUCTION

This book covers a number of aspects of data communications in some depth and this opening chapter gives an overview of data communication developments.

A new dimension was added to telecommunications when the need for information exchange between computers, and between remote terminals and host computers, began to materialize in the early 1960s. The Nationwide ubiquitous readily available telephone network provided a convenient vehicle for data transmission, and the invention of the modem enabled digital signals from computers to be converted into analogue form for transmission over the speech network. The telephone network that existed was designed for the economic transmission and switching of commercial quality speech, and a transmission bandwidth of 3kHz through the network was sufficient for a voice telephone call.

Fig 1.1 shows the three tier form of the telephone network, comprising of local cable access from customer to serving local telephone exchange, junction network interconnecting telephone exchanges in the same locality, and the main trunk network interconnecting cities and providing the long distance transmission. Analogue transmission with frequency division multiplexing was used in the main transmission network, and electromechanical step by step switching in the exchanges. Data transmission between computers and remote terminals could either use the public switch telephone network (PSTN) "2 wire" dial up connections, or alternatively permanently leased private circuits that only use the transmission elements of the network. The latter could be provided over 4 wire circuits with separate go and return channels end to end and permanent equalization to overcome circuit deficiencies. The use of Private Circuits became the popular method of connection, not only because of better performance and bandwidth that could be obtained, but also because most requirements for data communications were for within Company networks, with high traffic between nodes and no need to intercommunicate with other Companies' systems on an ad hoc basis.

Early modems were limited in performance and expensive. 300 bit/s full duplex or 1200 bit/s half duplex tended to be the highest speeds obtainable over 2 wire PSTN dial up connections. 2400, 4800 or 9600 full duplex modems gradually became available for use over 4 wire equalized Private Circuits. Speeds higher than these rates were not possible over normal voice circuits and, if required, customers had to rent the equivalent of twelve voice circuits, using special connections directly to main network frequency division multiplexing systems. Special cables were also required to extend these higher bandwidth systems to customer's premises.

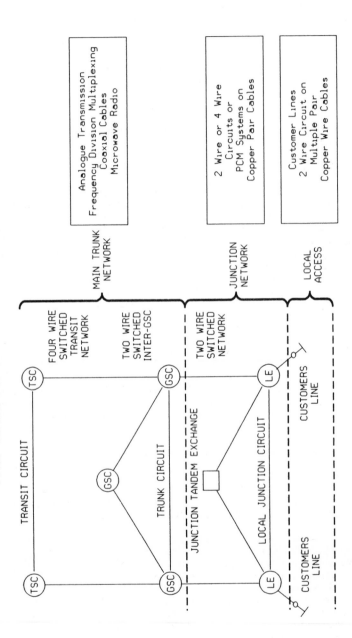

THE EXISTING TELEPHONE NETWORK

FIGURE 1.1

LE LOCAL EXCHANGE   GSC GROUP SWITCHING CENTRE   TSC TRANSIT SWITCHING CENTRE

We have witnessed a revolution in developments since those early days of the 1960s, both in the field of computers, terminals and consequent potential for new applications, as well as with modems. However, equally significant has been the revolutionary change in the structure and component parts of the telephone network itself, new technology enabling the introduction of digital transmission, time division multiplexing, pulse code modulation, and digital exchanges with time/space switching, computer controlled and with separate channel inter exchange signalling. These developments are already having a major impact on the opportunities for increased facilities, functionality, performance, and economies for data communication.

However, the most revolutionary network change which is only just beginning to make an impact is in the form of basic physical bearer plant used - optical fibres gradually replacing copper pair and coaxial cables in the network, and opening bandwidth capabilities hitherto unthought of.

Voice telephony will continue to be the majority service using the public network, and the economics of the telephone service must continue to determine the essential form and dimensions of the total public network. The digital transmission and switching elements now possible with today's technology, conveniently interface to form an integrated digital network (IDN) for voice telephony, which is significantly cheaper to install and maintain, than its analogue predecessor. Modernization of the telephone network is proceeding rapidly, and most major towns are now served by the new IDN. Digital transmission is used end to end between local exchanges in the IDN. Regeneration of the digitally encoded signals throughout the network ensures that quality is maintained end to end, and none of the cumulative distortion that was a product of the analogue system components occurs. With the IDN, analogue transmission is only used on the local extensions to customers premises. See Fig 1.2. In order that speech can be transmitted over the digital network it is necessary to convert the speech analogue signals to digital form at the local exchange using pulse code modulation systems. In order to ensure that a faithful acceptable replica of the speech signal is obtained in the Pulse Code Modulation process a 64 kbit/s coded digital line is necessary for each 4 kHz speech channel. This requirement has determined the "bandwidth" allocated for each telephone call or private circuit through the digital network, 64 kbit/s channels replacing the 3 kHz analogue channels that were the foundation of the old analogue network.

1.2   THE INTEGRATED SERVICES NETWORK (ISDN)

If, instead of converting the analogue signal to digital at the local exchanges, the digital path is extended out to customer's premises then it creates the possibility of a 64 kbit/s channel being available end to end from customer premises to customer premises. This 64 kbit/s capability forms the foundation of the integrated services digital network or ISDN. The availability of a full 64 kbit/s bandwidth on a normal telephone call provides significant additional opportunities compared with the traditional 9.6 kbit/s or 14.4 kbit/s obtainable by use of modems over an analogue PSTN call of 3 kHz bandwidth. The combination of this higher bandwidth, together with the high speed call set up capabilities of a modern digital telephone network, offer considerable opportunities for new applications. Whereas the setting up of a call in a step by step process through the old electromechanical exchanges would take on average 15 seconds, with the new digital telephone exchanges and modern signalling systems only a few hundred milliseconds are required. To take advantage of this fast signalling capability a new signalling protocol has been developed to enable customer's terminal equipment (either computer devices for data transmission or PBX exchanges), to communicate directly with the telephone network. To expand the customer service opportunities the ISDN access provides a second 64 kbit/s channel extended to the customer's premises. This enables the customer's terminal to set up two calls

MODERNISATION
THE INTEGRATED DIGITAL TRANSMISSION AND SWITCHING NETWORK (IDN)

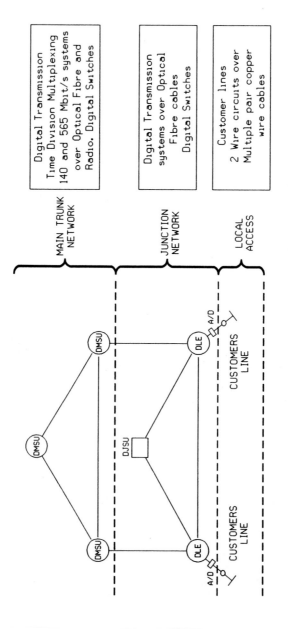

MAIN TRUNK NETWORK
- Digital Transmission Time Division Multiplexing 140 and 565 Mbit/s systems over Optical Fibre and Radio. Digital Switches

JUNCTION NETWORK
- Digital Transmission systems over Optical Fibre cables Digital Switches

LOCAL ACCESS
- Customer lines 2 Wire circuits over Multiple pair copper wire cables

DLE — LOCAL DIGITAL EXCHANGE

DJSU — DIGITAL JUNCTION SWITCHING UNIT

DMSU — DIGITAL MAIN SWITCHING UNIT

A/D — ANALOGUE TO DIGITAL CONVERSION EMBEDDED IN LOCAL EXCHANGE. CONVERTS ANALOGUE LOCAL ACCESS FROM CUSTOMER TO 64Kbit/s DIGITAL SIGNALS USING PCM

CUSTOMERS LINE

CUSTOMERS LINE

FIGURE 1.2

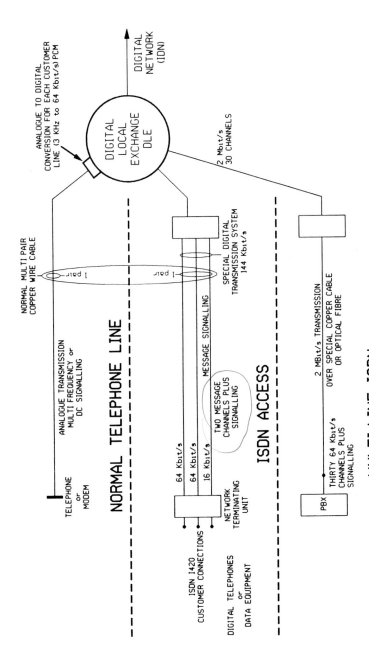

ANALOGUE TO DIGITAL CONVERSION FOR EACH CUSTOMER LINE (3 KHz to 64 Kbit/s) PCM

DIGITAL LOCAL EXCHANGE DLE

DIGITAL NETWORK (IDN)

2 Mbit/s 30 CHANNELS

NORMAL MULTI PAIR COPPER WIRE CABLE

1 pair

1 pair

SPECIAL DIGITAL TRANSMISSION SYSTEM 144 Kbit/s

MESSAGE SIGNALLING

ANALOGUE TRANSMISSION MULTI FREQUENCY or DC SIGNALLING

NORMAL TELEPHONE LINE

TELEPHONE or MODEM

64 Kbit/s
64 Kbit/s
16 Kbit/s

TWO MESSAGE CHANNELS PLUS SIGNALLING

ISDN ACCESS

NETWORK TERMINATING UNIT

ISDN 1420 CUSTOMER CONNECTIONS

DIGITAL TELEPHONES or DATA EQUIPMENT

2 MBit/s TRANSMISSION OVER SPECIAL COPPER CABLE OR OPTICAL FIBRE

MULTI LINE ISDN

PBX

THIRTY 64 Kbit/s CHANNELS PLUS SIGNALLING

FIGURE 1.3

independently to different destinations. The International Telephony Standards Committee (CCITT) has produced a recommended standard for the ISDN interface. This takes the form of 64 plus 64 plus 16 kbit/s access channels equaling 144 kbit/s total bandwidth of interface. This standard is known as CCITT recommendation I420. (See Fig 1.3) For those customers that require more than two circuits a second version of the CCITT recommendation provides for 30 64 kbit/s channels as well as a 64 kbit/s signalling channel. This interface enables modern PBXs designed for ISDN to interface directly with the digital network over a 2 Mbits/s transmission link.

1.3   ALTERNATIVES TO ISDN

Regardless of the bandwidth and technical performance capabilities of the ISDN, many data communications applications will continue to be better suited to point to point leased line connections, as are the majority at present, for the following reasons:

1   Many applications are tailor made or within Company operations and do not need to talk to other Companies systems.

2   The traffic is to and from a few or many outstations to one or two central host or database sites.

3   The traffic is high and links are well utilized.

British Telecom provides two key digital private circuit services built on the foundation of the modern digital telephone network. These are known as Megastream and Kilostream. Kilostream provides point to point digital leased lines at data rates of 2400, 4800, 9600, 48 kbit/s and 64 kbit/s, with X21 or X21BIS (V. compatible) interfaces. Therefore customers modems are not required. Megastream provides a full 2 Mbit/s capability which is mainly attractive to larger companies with major inter-site requirements. Fig 1.4 shows how the Kilostream service is provided, including the method of cross connection of 64 kbit/s channels strategically located points on the national network. Local end extensions to customer premises are provided over 2 wire normal copper wire local cables using WAL2 transmission. With this pre provided network service can be provided quickly from any of the network multiplexor sites, and special automatic cross connect switches are used at the nodal centres in order to enable quick set up and rerouting of the private circuits.

Extensive network management and network diagnostic facilities are included in the Kilostream service enabling continuous monitoring of the performance of multiplexor links, local ends and customer's premises sited Network Terminating Units (NTUs) for the 2.4, 4.8, 9.6 and 48 kbit/s end to end services.

In the old analogue network environment 48 kbit/s was considered a wideband service, because special network facilities needed to be extended to customer premises in order to provide this service. In the modernised digital environment the 2 Mbit/s Megastream service has now assumed that position. 2 Mbit/s end to end service (30 channel level of multiplexing in the public digital network hierarchy) is now available to offer to customers in most national locations. Most of BT's few thousand exchange sites are now accessible via 2 Mbit/s trunk transmission channel links which form the basic inter-exchange elements in the integrated digital network. 2 Mbit/s is not the limit of bandwidth capability available to customers in the future. Higher order bandwidths from the digital main network hierarchy will be available to those customers that are likely to require such transmission capacity between their sites (8, or 34, or 140 Mbit/s). The capabilities of Optical Fibre, already making a

REAM NETWORK

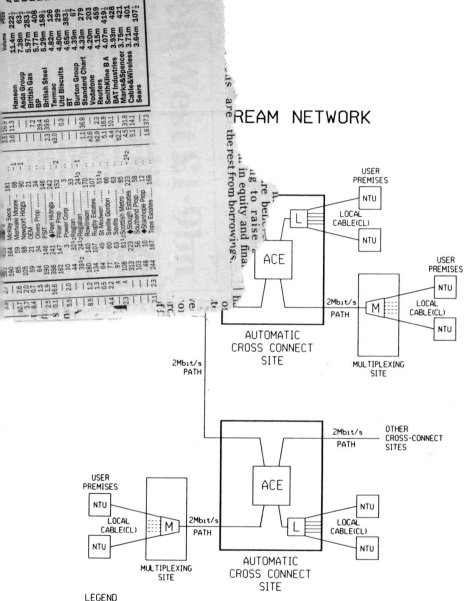

LEGEND

M - MULTIPLEXOR
NTU - NETWORK TERMINATING UNIT
L - LOCAL ACCESS EQUIPMENT
ACE - AUTOMATIC CROSS CONNECT EQUIPMENT any 64 Kbit/s channels derived from
      2 Mbit/s bearers can be interconnected

FIGURE 1.4

significant impact in the core network elements, when extended to customers premises will revolutionize bandwidth capabilities in the 1990s.

In the future the majority of PSTN (Switched Telephone Service) calls will continue to originate or be delivered to customer's premises in analogue form over 2 wire local ends, whilst a large proportion of the network, particularly that extending to overseas countries, will remain in analogue form. The use of the PSTN in general for dial up data calls is likely to increase as new computer applications result in a greater need for occasional calls to many different destinations on an ad hoc basis.   Data rates of 9600 bit/s Full Duplex and 14.4 kbit/s are now possible over analogue PSTN circuits.   This is because of recent revolutionary developments in analogue modems, and Fig 1.5 demonstrates the range now available.   Costs have decreased significantly, and the price of the sophisticated multilevel modulation, higher speed modems have converged on the price of the simpler lower speed modems.   Modems now often form an integral part of the terminal equipment, and include auto dialing and answering facilities as well as built-in fault diagnostic capabilities. Latest modems for PSTN dial up access to overlay networks such as Packet Switching, Prestel etc, offer automatic detection and training to different modulation rates and methods, thereby making better use of common dial up access circuits from the telephone network.

1.4   NETWORK MANAGEMENT

Network Management of Data Communication Networks has become increasingly important as more and more essential day to day business activities are committed to using on line computer systems.

Automatic loop back facilities for fault location are now becoming a standard feature within modems and multiplexors, together with central network management facilities which monitor and link together the facilities on the various network elements.

Multiplexor developments have equaled those in the modem field over the last 15 - 20 years. Early multiplexors were simple devices, allocating fixed channel bandwidths using frequency division multiplexing techniques.   Then followed the introduction of time division multiplexing and, for some applications, statistical multiplexing, and with these techniques possibilities for flexible and dynamic allocation of bandwidth.

The latest multiplexors are capable of sophisticated networking, are software controlled and configured, and include network management and diagnostic facilities. Multiplexors capable of handling aggregate bit streams of 2 Mbit/s or more are being used to interface with Megastream circuits to enable customers to integrate voice and data on the their major networks, and "drop and insert" facilities allow channels to be distributed efficiently around such a network. Network Management and control is a key feature in networks that are appearing in the digital environment.

1.5   HIGHER LEVELS OF PROTOCOL

So far in this Chapter, only the physical level of data communications has been considered, that is the facilities for transmission of binary bits across the network. At the physical level the network is not concerned with the block or message structure of the data, and the transmission links are fully transparent to the transfer of data.   The "physical" is the bottom layer in the ISO seven layer model concept introduced by the International Standards Organization (ISO).

SPEECH BAND MODEMS

Date Rate BIT/s	Public Switched Telephone Network (PSTN) or Private Circuits (PC)	CCITT Rec	Modulation Form	Full Duplex or Half Duplex	BT Modem
300	PSTN	V21	FSK	FD	4123X, 413X
1200	PSTN	V23	FSK	HD	4123X
1200	PSTN	V22	PSK	FD	4122X, 4124X*
2400	PSTN	V22bis	QAM	FD	4242
2400	PC (4-WIRE)	V26	PSK	FD	—
2400	PSTN	V26bis	PSK	HD	4241X
4800	PC (4-WIRE)	V27	PSK	FD	—
4800	PC (4-WIRE)	V27bis	PSK	FD	4480X
4800	PSTN	V27ter	PSK	HD	4480X
9600	PC (4-WIRE)	V29	QAM	FD	4960X
9600	PC (4-WIRE)	As V32 but no echo cancelling		FD	4961X
9600	PSTN/PC	V32	QAM	FD	4962X
14400	PC (4-WIRE)	V33	QAM	FD	4141X

FSK = Frequency Shift Keying
PSK = Phase Shift Keying
QAM = Quadrature Amplitude Modulation

* Includes V21 answer mode

FIGURE 1.5

ISO MODEL

LEVEL NUMBER	FUNCTION	EXAMPLES	RESPONSIBILITY
7	APPLICATION	DATABASE TIME SHARING ELECTRONIC FUNDS TRANSFER ORDER ENTRY	ISO
6	PRESENTATION CONTROL	DATA STRUCTURE FORMATS VIRTUAL TERMINAL PROTOCOL FILE TRANSFER PROTOCOL	ISO
5	SESSION CONTROL	SESSION MANAGEMENT	ISO
4	TRANSPORT END-TO-END	NETWORK INDEPENDENT INTERFACE	ISO
3	NETWORK CONTROL	X25 LEVEL 3 OR X21	CCITT
2	LINK CONTROL	X25 LEVEL 2 (LAPB)	CCITT
1	PHYSICAL CONTROL	X25 LEVEL 1 (X21 & X21 bis)	CCITT

NOTE 2

NOTE 1

HIGHER LEVEL PROTOCOLS

STANDARD TRANSPORT SERVICE

STANDARD NETWORK SERVICE

NOTES : 1. ISO for private networks
2. CCITT for Network Services (ISO collaboration)

FIGURE 1.6

1.6 NETWORK ARCHITECTURE - THE ISO SEVEN LAYER MODEL

The Telecoms Administrations first venture into providing other than "wires only" bit transparent systems brought the influence of CCITT as well as International Standards Organization (ISO) into the computer world. Until that time CCITT's influence had stopped at the V series modem interface or X21 NTU interface. The OSI seven layer protocol model and open system working emerged. (See Fig 1.6)

The concept of the OSI seven layer model is that each layer has a defined interface with those above and below, but is not concerned with how the services it uses from the lower layers are carried out, or the way the services it performs for higher layers are used. Each layer can therefore be developed independently, as long as it meets the requirements of the adjacent layers' interfaces.

The final objective is to achieve standardization at all seven levels so that Open System working between different customers terminals and systems can be achieved.

Network Architecture - The Lower Levels

1.6.1 The Physical Level
[CCITT Recommendations X.21 and X.21 bis].

Modern applications developed for use over data communication networks are designed with the architectural model of the network always in mind. Within the ISO model the Physical Level offers the network links only in terms of bit transmission, in the case of analogue modems the V24 or V35 interfaces, and in the case of digital NTU's X21 or X21 bis (V compatible) interfaces. These interfaces provide transmit and receive wires for binary digital data transmission together with, in the case of synchronous operation, bit timing for synchronization purposes. This forms the bottom layer of the OSI model.

1.6.2 The Link Level
[CCITT Recommendations X.25 LAPB]

The next level of protocol in a data transmission system is concerned with link control. The terminals at the end of a link need to exchange meaningful information to format the live data into groups or blocks for checking of successful transmission over the link, retransmission if necessary, and flow control.

In the early days of data communication "Basic Mode" was introduced. This designated certain IA5 characters for essential network functions such as acknowledgement - ACK, negative acknowledgement - NACK etc. The system was simple and flexible for both asynchronous and synchronous data transmission, but lacked transparency and had limitations for error checking.

More recently HDLC (Higher Level Data Link Control) has been developed. In this system data is grouped into blocks, each block preceded by a header, and ending with the sum check of an error detection algorithm, that can be processed by the receiving station. Data within the block is transparent. There are variants of HDLC procedures by different computer system suppliers, but it is now forming the recognized basis for link level protocol on many systems.

12 Introduction

1.6.3 The Network Control Level
[CCITT Recommendations X.21 and X.25]

The next level in the seven layer model is the "Network Level". In a switched network operation there is a need to communicate between terminals and the network switches. In the simple PSTN operation this is done by 'dial up' signals which can either be manually generated or produced by processors. With this simple system no further signalling takes place during the data phase, except for the clear down condition.

CCITT Recommendation X21 protocol was introduced to enable terminals to signal to switches in a dedicated circuit switched data network. It has two separate status conditions - signalling and data transmission - which are indicated over the terminal to network X21 interfaces by means of conditions on signalling wires. This status condition is then conveyed over the network by means of an extra bit outside the 6 or 8 bits used for data.

Characters for signalling are then taken from the IA5 set. Byte timing is therefore also required across the X21 interface in order to provide demarcation of characters.

Therefore with circuit switched network (whether PSTN or dedicated), the network provides a transparent bitstream capability not concerned with the content of the data or any error checking process (which must be performed terminal to terminal if required).

Packet switching is a technique that has developed since the early 1970s and has raised much interest regarding its potential for certain applications. Moving on from the experiments of the 1970s we have witnessed small operational public networks being introduced in most major countries, together with the development of an inter-network protocol X75, has facilitated the establishment of an international infrastructure of inter-linked national packet networks.

With packet switching a circuit or channel of fixed bandwidth is not maintained between caller and called terminal for the duration of a call. Instead data is transmitted in packets each with a header containing address information, and a tail containing error check sum information. Bandwidth is allocated dynamically on the network links as required. (See Fig 1.7)

The advantages of packet switching are:

1   More efficient use is made of the transmission links - both inter-network and customer to network.

2   Many calls can take place simultaneously, to and from different destinations, over the same customer to network physical link.

3   Error checking is provided on a line basis within the network, and from network to customer using HDLC link protocol.

4   The inherent buffering in the system enables terminals of different speeds to interwork.

The penalties incurred for the above advantages are:

1   More complicated switches.

2   A fairly complicated network to customer protocol that has to be implemented in customer terminals and network, and which is not necessarily tuned to all application requirements.

COMPARISON OF PACKET SWITCHING AND CIRCUIT SWITCHING

Circuit Switching

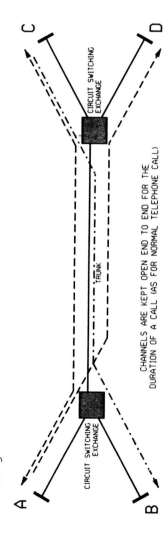

CHANNELS ARE KEPT OPEN TO END FOR THE
DURATION OF A CALL (AS FOR NORMAL TELEPHONE CALL)

Packet Switching

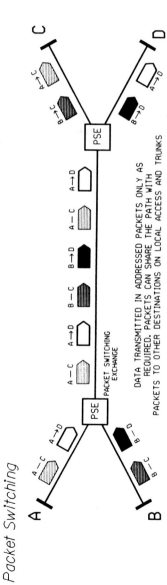

DATA TRANSMITTED IN ADDRESSED PACKETS ONLY AS
REQUIRED. PACKETS CAN SHARE THE PATH WITH
PACKETS TO OTHER DESTINATIONS ON LOCAL ACCESS AND TRUNKS

FIGURE 1.7

3   Variable delay according to the level of traffic and resultant queuing in
the system.

Packet switching is recognized as having advantages for certain types of
application, even in an ISDN environment where the "ISDN PSTN"
can offer 64 kbit/s high bandwidth circuit switching capability. Packet
Switching can handle short duration, interactive low content messages, to
and from many destinations more economically, and Electronic Funds
Transfer (EFT) is such an example ideally suited to packet switching.

The X25 protocol embraces levels 1, 2 and 3 of the OSI seven layer
model, and provides the HDLC link control and error protection at
Level 2, and the network signalling, call routing, logical channel
multiplexing and flow control at Level 3.   To avoid the need for simple
single channel terminals to implement the packet protocol, Packet
Assembly Disassembly (PAD) facilities are provided as an additional
interface to packet networks.   A popular application of this is to provide
local dial up access over the PSTN from simple terminals to a network
PAD function. From there the data is transmitted in packet form.
What about the future of packet switching? It has now gained a certain
critical mass worldwide, and there is no doubt that it is well suited to
certain applications. Much depends upon the influence of future
network economics in a fully digital environment, and the continuing
reduction in cost of terminal equipment and the sophistication that can be
built therein.   Packet   switching   provided   the   catalyst   for
development of   a discipline in dealing with the possibilities of
interworking between different terminals and systems.   Hitherto, for
commercial expediency, computer suppliers had developed their own
particular systems, tailor made for specific operations.
Apart from some changes to add functionality the lower level Wide Area
Network (WAN) protocols (eg X25) have remained stable for the past
four years. This has not been the case for Lower Level Local Area Network
(LAN) technology and the associated standards which have advanced at a
tremendous rate.   In   particular the advent of powerful but cheap
'intelligence' in the network has allowed new approaches to system design
and structure previously unavailable to the network designer.
Also in considering network developments one cannot ignore the impact that
advances in digital technology have had on terminal developments, and the
consequent effects on the relative roles of networks and terminals in a
complete system.
In the early days of data communications, terminals were simple in
capability, but needed to be complicated mechanical devices in order to
perform that capability, and were consequently relatively expensive.
Transmit and receive, characters were handled synchronously and
printed one at a time on paper or punched tape.
Electronic devices were then developed with some local memory, and
limited local processing capability including local editing and formatting
capabilities.
Then followed the introduction of "Frame Mode" synchronous
terminals, with a capability for displaying formatted data tailored for
specific applications.   Finally, the introduction of the personal computer,
and new dimensions in local memory capability, floppy disks and
Winchester discs, has revolutionized the possibilities for local processing,
formatting and display, including sophisticated graphics capabilities.
Terminal power and economics are now such that many functions are
largely independent of main frames and networks, and features which a few

years ago were being built into networks are now more conveniently provided in terminals.
What a few years ago seemed like a complex protocol, requiring a considerable portion of a main frame computer is now implemented on a 'plug in' PC card.
The development of LANs has followed the same path as WANs in that various protocols and physical standards have developed in parallel. Most are now covered in the ISO 8802.X series. Whilst initially developed as inter-PC communications systems LANs now form component parts of major computer systems (eg DEC and ICL). With the imminent introduction of fibre optic LAN standards, LAN applications still have even more scope to develop.
A typical 4 Mbit/s LAN (soon to be upgraded to 16 Mbits/s) can support hundreds of intelligent workstations, personal computers (PCs) and storage and communications devices without any of the delays or limits a WAN would impose. Physical distance will not be a limiting factor for long. The use of high speed digital links (eg Megastream) and remote 'Bridges' allow the interconnection of LANs offering the concept of a national 'Wide Area' LAN.

Network Architecture - The Upper Levels

The last few years has also seen the development of higher level protocols at an ever increasing pace. More than 10 major High Level Protocols were ratified in 1988 alone.

1.6.4 The Transport Level
[ISO 8072, CCITT Recommendations X.214 and X.224]

The bottom three layers of the OSI model, outlined above, are concerned with the physical, link and network signalling functions, whilst the fourth "Transport Level" provides the network independent bridge between the terminal function and network. The Transport level caters for the fact that terminals and terminal applications may interface with a variety of network types, Circuit switched, Packet switched, etc.
Of the top three levels PTTs have little direct influence in development and much falls outside the domain of CCITT. The subject itself is more complex than the more easily defined requirements at the network levels. The pressures from the computer supply industry for commercial expediency are considerable, and a number of effective self contained systems from major computer suppliers have, because of the major investments involved, become competitors for de facto standards. Furthermore it must be remembered that the majority of customers data processing applications do not need to talk to those of other businesses.

1.6.5 The Session Level
[ISO 8326, Recommendations X.215 and X.225]

The Session Level protocols link separate transactions associated with the same application. Once a session is established (normally by a 'Log on' or identity sequence) then it is maintained even if no data is being exchanged. The session is closed when all work associated with the application is complete (or security imposes an in-activity forced logoff). A session might be established at start of work and closed at end of day.

A MESSAGE HANDLING SERVICE BASED ON CCITT REC X400

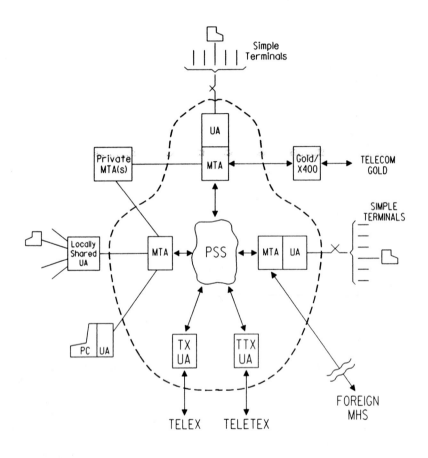

MTA = Message transfer agents (store and forward message exchanges)
UA = User agents (interface with user for message preparation and handling)

FIGURE 1.8

1.6.6   The Presentation Level
[ISO 8823, CCITT Recommendations X.216 and X.226]

To provide Open System services it is necessary that a user 'sees' information presented in the same form even when systems come from different suppliers.   Definitions   for   screen presentation (ie size, colour, number of lines, scroll mode etc) if agreed by all suppliers then form an agreed set which the top layer (application) can use and rely on.

1.6.7   The Application Level

Just two examples of the highest levels of protocol are:

1.   CCITT   Recommendation X.400 - Message Handling   Systems (MHS), see Fig 1.8. The CCITT X400 messaging service visualizes component units built into the networks for storing and forwarding of messages, protocol conversion etc.

2.   ISO 8571 - File Transfer Access and Management (FTAM). This major   standard covers topics such as types of data transfer, file management, document types and error recovery.

1.7   CONCLUSIONS

This Chapter has attempted to give an   overview of data communication network developments in the UK on the existing PSTN and analogue leased lines, new digital leased line services and the introduction of ISDN, together with the specialized application of packet switching and its past influence and future potential. All   these elements must be seen as part of the emergence of the 7 Level model in its drive to support applications requiring inter-communication between different customers' systems, and the move towards open system working.
There will continue to be an increasing need for large private networks as more and more companies become dependent on real time processing systems for business applications linking remote sites.
Applications for Local Area Networks will also expand as terminal costs for a given sophistication continue to fall making the office of the future a reality for the 1990s.
There is no doubt that the most radical change that will   occur will result from the tremendous   bandwidth capabilities offered by optical fibre. During the previous twenty or more years of data communications history developments have been constrained by network limitations.   The situation is now changing, and already ISDN can offer more bandwidth that most terminals can handle - 64 kbit/s or 8000 characters a second. The cost of pure bit transport must eventually fall to a fraction of present day costs.
The key to maximizing all this potential in the future lies in maintaining the recent momentum that has been established towards standardization through CCITT and ISO. will always be the need to balance the drive of innovation and the interests of commercial expediency against the wider benefits of standardization. The last 20 years have seen the results of tremendous dedication and hard work in standards organizations to keep pace with the potential of technology and meet the needs of emerging applications. Competition offers much scope for early release of new products and services at attractive prices, but it must not be at the expense of the longer term development of a sound national and international telecoms infrastructure, capable of providing open system working with acceptable levels of network performance end to end.

Chapter 2

Data Communication Systems - An Overview

John T.L. Sharpe

2.1   INTRODUCTION

The widespread development of data communication systems - the data communication revolution - has been driven by the ever-increasing use of computers in many diverse applications in industry, commerce and, more latterly, the home. For a long time stand-alone computers provided an invaluable facility in scientific and data processing work, but over the years, because of changing economics and patterns of usage in computing, there has developed the need for people to communicate with remote computers, and also for computer to communicate with computer. It has therefore become steadily more apparent that it is the merging of the two technologies of telecommunications and computing that will make the greatest economic and social impact in society. Data transmission technology is the key to achieving this.

The objective of this chapter is to provide an overview of the nature and shape of typical data communication systems used today, to discuss briefly both the systems and implementation technologies that are employed in their realization and to put all these factors into an overall perspective. Subsequent chapters will elaborate in more detail on specific systems of particular commercial importance and on the most significant aspects of data communications base technology.

2.2   THE CHARACTERISTICS OF DATA

One can broadly distinguish three basic types of information, categorized by source, which it may be required to transmit through a telecommunications network:

-- Speech
-- Video
-- Data

Of these, speech is by far the most important at the present time, and its transmission requirements have, up until very recently, determined virtually all the characteristics of our national telecommunication networks. In terms of the requirements for network transmission capacity, speech will remain the dominant form of traffic for the foreseeable future. Speech signals are redundant and robust and can withstand the effects of considerable additive noise and waveform distortion without significant degradation in intelligibility

Video transmission is the sleeping giant of telecommunications. Transmission of TV standard video requires a bandwidth of 5-6MHz. If the viewphone concept ever takes off in a big way, the impact on the transmission capacity requirements of telecommunication networks will be enormous. Currently, however, there is not a lot of broadcast TV programme material, and cable TV and teleconferencing are growing areas.

Speech and video are real-time signals, and therefore need to be transmitted and processed in real time. By contrast, no such teal time constraints apply to data: it is therefore possible, and frequently more convenient, to transmit data using a packet switching technique instead of the more conventional circuit switching which is used for speech, and necessary for any real time type information. Thus, in the planning of data transmission services, much attention has been given to developing packet type interfaces to networks, resulting in CCITT Recommendations X.3, X.25, X.28, X.29 and X.75.

2.3   THE TRANSMISSION MEDIA

The transmission channel provides the means for interconnecting nodes in a network. There are a variety of different transmission media which may be used, and these can be classified as either 'bounded' or unbounded'. The following are examples of transmission media that are used for data transmission:

Bounded Media	Unbounded Media
Optical Fibre	Radio
Coaxial Cable	Infra Red
Telephone Network	Ultrasonics
Wire Pairs	
TELEX Network	
Electricity Supply Wiring	

There is a very important basic difference between bounded and unbounded media: in the former case, the bandwidth, and hence transmission capacity of a network can, in principle, be increased indefinitely by adding further cables or fibres. However, in the case of unbounded media, the communications bandwidth within the range of a group of transmitters is limited. This situation can be considerably improved by careful choice of transmitter power and area coverage as in the case of cellular radio systems, but there still remains a finite upper limit to the capacity of such a network.

The characteristics of these different kinds of transmission media vary considerably and are summarized in the following paragraphs.

2.3.1   Optical Fibres

These are characterized by wide bandwidth, maximum bit rates being typically of the order of hundreds of Mb/s. They are immune to electromagnetic interference and conversely do not generate interference themselves, and consequently find an application in electrically noisy industrial environments. Optical fibres are used in the trunk telephone network and in local area networks for interconnecting computers.

2.3.2 Coaxial Cables

These are used for high speed point-to-point links and for local area networks. Maximum speeds are of the order tens of Mb/s, depending upon the type of cable and the transmitter and receiver circuit technique used.

2.3.3 The Telephone Network

Data transmission access to the telephone network is usually via a modem which carries out the signal conversion necessary to make the data signals compatible with the transmission characteristics of the telephone network. Using this approach, data rates of up to 16 or 19.2 kb/s can be achieved. For higher speeds, access to p.c.m. transmission facilities by means of BT Kilostream and Megastream services provides rates of 64 kb/s and 2 Mb/s respectively. The introduction, over the next few years, of the Integrated Services Digital Network (ISDN), will make directly available at the subscriber terminals channels with data rates of 2 x 64 kb/s and 16 kb/s, which will make data communication a much simpler process.

2.3.4 Wire Pairs

Wire pairs are used for short distance data communication at low speeds, up to a few tens of Kb/s, typically for connecting computer peripherals to modems and computer systems.

2.3.5 TELEX Network

The TELEX Network is the oldest public data communication facility, with transmission parameters that were originally based on the performance capabilities of mechanical teleprinters. It uses 50 b/s stop-start transmission, with a conversational type protocol, is widely available internationally and is very useful in business, as with answerbacks appended it is accepted as a legal document with proof of delivery.

2.3.6 Electricity Supply Wiring

Short distance, in-site data communication is possible using the mains wiring as a transmission medium together with special modems. Transmission speeds of 1200 b/s have been used successfully. This approach has the merit of not requiring any additional cabling to support the information transmission: it is useful in electricity supply control applications and in cases where the provision of separate cabling is either expensive or impossible.

2.3.7 Radio Systems

Radio links are a difficult medium for data communications because they are subject to fading and other time-varying instabilities of various kinds. These can have a duration which is long in comparison with a bit period, and thus have a serious effect on the error rate. In spite of these drawbacks, this medium is assuming considerable commercial importance with the rapid development of cellular radio systems. In addition to data communication over mobile radio, the various paging systems that are in operation are examples of the use of radio for data communications. A rather different kind of service which sends data over a radio channel is TELETEXT, of which the Ceefax and Oracle services operated by the BBC and IBA are examples. Another similar application is DATACAST, the bulk data transmission service which is currently being proposed by the BBC.

2.3.8 Infra-Red Channels

These are used for short distance transmission where the use of wires is impossible or inconvenient, for example TV set remote control and 'wireless' coupling of keyboards to terminals and computers (e.g. IBM PCjn personal computer).

2.3.9. Ultrasonic Channels

These fill a similar slot to infra-red transmission, but with a greater range and less "line of sight" constraint and find application in remote control using transmission through the air. In addition, ultrasonics are used in underwater data communication applications, such as communication between unmanned submersibles or mini-subs, and the mother ship on the surface, as well as having a variety of military applications.

2.4 NETWORK CONFIGURATIONS

Network configurations, or topologies as they are frequently called, are created by the particular geometric arrangement of links (communication channels) and nodes (data sinks and/or sources) that make up the network.

There are about six different basic topologies which can be used for constructing networks: point-to-point, multidrop, star, ring, bus and mesh. These will now be considered briefly.

2.4.1 Point-to-Point Links

This is the simplest network configuration and consists of just two nodes.

2.4.2 Multidrop or Multipoint Links

The multidrop link is a single channel shared by more than two nodes and is used to reduce the number of channels required in a network, and thereby reduce the cost. This, of course, is only possible if a single line can support the required level of traffic.

2.4.3 Star Networks

Here all the nodes are joined at a single central point. This network configuration is particularly suited to situations where most of the traffic is between the central and outlying nodes. Examples are a PABX or a cluster of terminals connected to a central computer.

2.4.4 Ring Systems

The distinguishing feature of a ring network is that all the nodes are connected together in the form of a continuous circular configuration. Transmitted information travels around the ring from node to node and is picked off by the destination node.

2.4.5 Bus Systems

The bus topology consists of a single channel which is shared by a number of nodes, and functions in a similar way to a multidrop circuit. The term "bus system", however, is normally reserved for local and small area networks, whereas "multidrop" usually refers to systems set up on the telephone network. Ethernet is the best example of a widely used bus system.

2.4.6 Mesh Networks

In describing anything as flexible as a network configuration it is necessary to have some catch-all phrase which covers everything which does not conveniently fit in to any of the other simply defined categories. This is met by the term 'mesh network', or 'unconstrained topology' as it is sometimes called.

There are two other types of sub-system which are of considerable importance in data networks. These are multiplexers and network management systems (NMS).

Complex networks have spawned another communications related product area - the network management system. Originally conceived in the USA to help overcome the "finger pointing" problems that inevitably arose when there was an equipment malfunction in networks spanning three or four different carriers and equipment suppliers, they are now an essential component of modern data communication networks because of the tremendous reliance that is placed upon computer communication by modern business and industry. The present generation of intelligent NMS's incorporate facilities for monitoring link performance and giving an early warning of anticipated equipment failure. They can also be used to collect and provide traffic statistics which can be used for planning network upgrades and extensions.

Multiplexers combine a number of low speed data channels into a single higher speed channel, thereby achieving economies in the number of links required in a network and producing corresponding cost savings.

2.5 DATA COMMUNICATION SYSTEM TECHNOLOGY

The key technology areas in data communications are:

-- Signal Design (including modulation and signal shaping)
-- Timing Extraction (bit and word)
-- Signal Detection (including demodulation and adaptive equalization)
-- Error Control

2.5.1 Signal Design

Signal design can be defined as the design of the overall spectral shape of the transmitted signal. This includes the transmitter bandlimiting filters, the modulation system and the receiver noise-limiting filters. This topic was given extensive study in the 1960's - the early days of data modems - and the design implications for most types of channel are well understood. Signal shaping must be optimized to minimize intersymbol interference (the effect of pulse dispersion due to bandlimiting) and the effects of additive noise.

2.5.2 Timing Extraction

Timing extraction is the most difficult problem in digital transmission and for a long time was a rather neglected one. Reliable clock extraction from highly dispersed signals is essential for high speed digital transmission over some media, and is made more difficult in the case of digital implementation. Satisfactory algorighms were eventually developed, albeit of some complexity.

2.5.3 Signal Detection

This is taken to include demodulation of the received signal, plus any adaptive equalization that may be used to correct waveform distortion which has occurred because of the non-ideal characteristics of the transmission medium. Algorithms for carrier recovery and adaptive equalizers are now well understood. In the last few years, a new class of detection algorithms has been developed which involve soft-decision processes: degenerate Viterbi algorithms. These can offer an improved performance over conventional adaptive equalization because they use more of the available information from the received signal than a simple sample and slice detector.

2.5.4 Error Control

Error control by coding the data prior to transmission and introducing some element of redundancy according to the coding algorithm, enables the system designer to effect a trade-off between data rate and error rate. Considerable study has been devoted to the development of a variety of coding algorithms which are optimum under various conditions, for example, random errors or burst errors. The criterion of coding effectiveness is the ratio of performance improvement to percentage of added redundancy.

2.6 TECHNOLOGY FOR THE IMPLEMENTATION OF DATA COMMUNICATION SYSTEMS

On the implementation side of data communication systems there are three technologies which are making a significant impact:

-- Semiconductor Technology

-- Development of Layered Architectures for Communication Systems

-- Optical Communication

2.6.1 Semiconductor Technology

Compared with telecommunications, the history of the development of integrated circuit technology has been brief but dramatic. Since the development of the metal oxide-semiconductor (MOS) transistor in the late 1950's, through the late 1970's, device complexity doubled every year. The primary reasons for this growth rate were larger die size, higher density (smaller line widths on the silicon), and advances in device design. Since 1979, the growth rate in IC complexity has slowed down to doubling every 1.5 to 2 years. This is because technological limits were being approached, particularly in the case of devices with regular structures, such as memory chips, and to the fact that it is not yet clear how designers can best make effective use of the ability to design random-logic integrated circuits containing hundreds of thousands of transistors, to develop highly marketable, general-purpose chips.

The growth in viable complexity per chip has a direct effect on the cost of integrated circuits. The cost of LSI integrated circuits consists of two major components: silicon chip cost and assembly/test cost. For given design techniques and process technology, the chip cost is roughly an exponential function of complexity. Conversely, the assembly/test cost component can, as a first approximation, be considered as independent of complexity. By combining these two components, the cost per function will have a minimum corresponding to the optimum complexity for the current state of the art technology. As time moves on, better techniques will improve chip circuit density, and the chip cost will decrease. Thus, the optimum cost per function will decrease with time and allow more and more of a system to economically fit on a single integrated circuit. In addition, the smaller line widths that give increased component densities also result in an increase in the speed of operation of the chip (clock-rate). Since the processing clock-rate, cost per computation function has decreased exponentially. Table 4.1 illustrates the past and anticipated development of chip complexity.

Table 4.1

Year	Die Area (sq mm)	Minimum Line Width	Transistors per Chip
1960	1	30	22
1970	2.5	10	1,250
1980	6	3	80,000
1990	10	0.5	5,000,000

These developments have two effects on the data communication business. Firstly,. the resulting very low cost of computing power makes distributed intelligence possible in the broadest sense, with widespread local processing capabilities that all require the ability to interact with other intelligent systems by means of data communications. Secondly, cheap IC's mean low cost hardware and the cost of implementing data communications systems is correspondingly decreased, or alternatively, more complex, smarter systems become economically justified. Compare, for example, the dumb modems of the 1960's with the smart, user-friendly multi-speed devices with built-in diagnostics that are available today. Similar observations would also apply to terminals.

2.6.2 Layered Architectures for Communication Systems

The problems of connecting systems together are all basically variants of the familiar "pin connection problem" - what signal goes down which piece of wire and when. The more complex the system and the interface, then the greater is the potential for possible horrendous confusion and frustration when attempting to connect two pieces of equipment together - a fact only too well known to most engineers, whether dealing with a personal computer or an international computer network. Distributed processing requires a meaningful co-operation between the corresponding elements in a distributed system to perform an information processing task. This co-operation can only be made possible by using communication protocols which specify the sequences of interactions that are used to communicate about the task, together with their formats and meanings.

The systems of different manufacturers frequently use different conventions for representing information: they will differ in both their internal character codes and methods of representing numerical data. There are also many different conventions for representing information intended for driving printers and display devices, test-systems, message transfer systems and innumerable other application specific systems.

Thus, in practice, because of this proliferation of different manufacturers' conventions, system interconnection is frequently complicated considerably by the fact that like elements may not exist in the systems to be interconnected, and because each system uses its own conventions for information representation and control codes. In this situation, there can be no predetermined understanding between systems, and effective communication becomes impossible. To achieve the goal of intercommunication in these circumstances it is necessary to develop a sub-system known as a "gateway" - a black box interposed in the communications path, which converts the information representation conventions of one system into those of the other. Always assuming, of course, that it is possible to make an effective mapping of the constructs and commands of one system upon those of the other. However, the number of different types of gateway required in a network is roughly proportional to the square of the number of different types of system involved, so that this can be a cumbersome and expensive solution to pursue when the number of different systems to be interconnected becomes large.

In 1978, as a start to developing some order out of the system interconnection chaos, the International Standards Organization (ISO) issued a recommendation for a model for network architecture, known as the ISO model for Open Systems Interconnection. The OSI model, as it has become known, is made up of seven layers. The layers are functionally independent of each other, and each provides a certain subset of the functions required for system interconnection. They can thus be changed and enhanced, or cost-reduced without affecting other layers, something that is very important for adapting as painlessly as possible to the continuing advances in implementation and system technologies and user requirements.

2.6.3 Optical Communications

Fibre optic communications became a viable proposition in the late 1960's. Since that time, rapid progress has been made in terms of cost/Km, bit-rate and repeater spacing. The basic elements of an optical communication system are the fibre itself, the optical source and the optical detector: fibre optic technology is developing rapidly in all these three areas, and it can be confidently expected that the cost of providing bandwidth with the transmission medium will continue to reduce, with consequent continued movement in the cost cross-over between copper and fibre.

The impact of fibre optic communication technology on data communications is due to its potential to provide wide bandwidth links at low cost. Fibre optics currently find the greatest and most ready application in local area networks (LAN's), and a number of fibre optic LAN's have already appeared on the market. As well as providing a high data throughput, the very high bandwidth is utilized to make the transport process more transparent to the user, by minimizing network access and queuing times, which means that in distributed systems, users can effectively be completely divorced from the geographical separation between system units.

2.7 THE FUTURE

Data will never be a dominant force in determining the shape of future telecommunication networks, since in comparison with speech and the potential of video, its demands in terms of transmission capacity are small. It is reasonable to suppose, therefore, that data transmission requirements will normally be superimposed on other services, as in the case of the ISDN proposals, TELETEXT on broadcast TV, and PRESTEL on the present speech network.

What then, will determine the future trends in data communication? Essentially there appear to be six principle factors.

a)   It is cheaper, and usually more convenient, to move information around rather than people.

b)   Terminal system costs will continue to decrease.

The cost of hardware will continue to decrease due to continuing progress in semiconductor technology. Software costs will also decrease, over a somewhat longer timescale, due to better software development management techniques, and by improved software re-usability brought about by more widespread adoption of the ISO layered approach to system architecture.

c)   The cost of bandwidth will decrease.

The introduction of ISDN, giving better bandwidth utilization of the subscribers loop, the use of fibre optic transmission and the use of broadcast radio and TV channels for data will be the contributing factors here.

d)   The cost of labour, despite current economic conditions, will continue to rise

This will continue the trend in automation of labour-intensive processes, which in many cases will involve the introduction of a data communications element.

e)   Location-independent communications.

The current surge of interest in radio communications in the form of pagers and mobile phones will stimulate the need for communication at any place and at any time. Because of the inherent limitation on the total bandwidth available with an unbounded medium such as radio, there will be a tendency to use date communication, rather than speech, because of its much lower bandwidth requirements.

f)   The trend towards distributed, rather than centralized intelligence in communication systems.

The considerable reductions in the cost of processing power that have taken place in the last few years means that it is no longer necessary to concentrate all network intelligence in large centralized switching systems. Intelligence can be distributed throughout the network with consequent benefits in reliability and also to the complexity of management problems (and associated high cost) of developing large switching machines.

Data communications will continue to grow in importance. Lower costs, for both hardware and bandwidth, together with the greater availability of computers and storage devices will mean that during the next few years, data transmission will become almost as widespread and common-place as speech transmission is today.

Chapter 3

Principles of Data Transmission

Dr. Ron Brewster

3.1 INTRODUCTION

Data transmission is the process of communicating information in digital form from one location to another. If the communication is simply between two terminals in reasonably close geographical proximity, then there is really no problem in providing a dedicated connection with adequate bandwidth and suitably chosen characteristics to enable direct interconnection to be made. Difficulties arise, however, where there are several terminals that need to be interconnected so that communication can take place between any pair (or more) of terminals, or where the distances involved, and the usage is such, that it is uneconomic to provide dedicated special-purpose circuits.

3.2 THE BASIC PROBLEMS OF LONG DISTANCE DATA TRANSMISSION

If data transmission systems consisted only of short lengths of properly matched coaxial cable, there would be little difficulty in digital data transmission. The output waveform from such a channel is virtually identical to the input waveform. However, when data is sent over networks which have not been designed with data transmission on mind, such as the public telephone network, the transmission path may differ from the ideal in the following ways:

3.2.1 Restricted bandwidth.

Frequency components beyond some upper limit are heavily attenuated by the channel. The effect of a limited high frequency response on a binary waveform is illustrated in fig.3.1a.

3.2.2 No d.c. Response

Frequency components below some limit may be heavily attenuated, with no transmission at all at zero frequency. The effect of limited low frequency response on a binary waveform is illustrated in fig.3.1b.

3.2.3 Gain-Frequency and Phase-Frequency distortion.

The gain of a channel will vary to some extent even between the lower and upper cut-off frequencies. This results in the output waveform differing from the input waveform because the frequency components have had their amplitudes changed by differing amounts. Similarly, if the phase-shift versus frequency characteristic of the channel deviates from a straight line (i.e. transmission delay varies with frequency), the frequency components are delayed by differing amounts, so that the output waveform differs from the input waveform. The effect of gain-frequency and phase-frequency distortion on a binary waveform is illustrated in fig.3.1c.

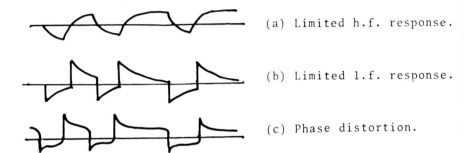

(a) Limited h.f. response.

(b) Limited l.f. response.

(c) Phase distortion.

Fig.3.1 Effects of various degradations on binary data.

3.2.4 Echoes

Discontinuities in the transmission path cause reflections of the transmitted signals which occur at the receiver as signal echoes.

3.2.5 Additive Gaussian Noise

Any transmission system incorporating amplifiers will introduce random noise, added to the signal waveform. In a telephone system, such noise can be heard as background hiss. This noise usually has zero d.c. value and an approximately Gaussian amplitude distribution. The Gaussian distribution curve is given in fig.3.2. For a given r.m.s. noise level, there is some particular probability that the signal plus noise will appear closer to the value for an incorrect symbol than to the value for the correct one. Noise will thus cause a proportion of the symbols received to be in error. Note that, because the Gaussian distribution tails off very rapidly, the error rate diminishes very rapidly indeed with increase in signal-to-noise ratio.

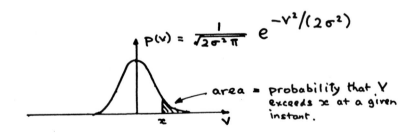

$$p(v) = \frac{1}{\sqrt{2\sigma^2 \pi}} \, e^{-v^2/(2\sigma^2)}$$

area = probability that V exceeds x at a given instant.

Fig.3.2 Gaussian Curve

3.2.6 Burst Noise

Some transmission systems suffer from occasional bursts of high amplitude noise such as clicks and pops in telephone systems or ignition interference in radio systems. normally all symbols occurring during such noise bursts are lost.

3.2.7 Other degradations

The foregoing transmission impairments are the ones that normally give difficulty in practice. Other types of degradation exist and may give trouble in special circumstances. These include non-linear transmission characteristics due, for example, to amplifier overload, frequency off-sets in f.d.m. systems and time-varying channel characteristics such as encountered in h.f. radio and underwater data transmission.

3.3. THE IDEAL CHANNEL

The two transmission limitations that set a fundamental limit to the rate at which data can be transmitted are noise and restricted bandwidth. Information theory (Shannon [1]) shows that, if a channel has a bandwidth of W Hz and a signal power to noise power ratio r, data can, in principle, be reliably transmitted at a rate C given by:

$$C = W \log_2 (1 + r) \text{ bits/ second.}$$

However, this is a theoretical upper limit that cannot be reached in practice. In practical systems, the transmission rate is, invariably, a fraction of the rate given by this formula. The ideal channel has constant gain from zero to infinite frequency, no phase-frequency distortion, no noise and no other transmission impairments. If we assume synchronous transmission, every T units of time a short high amplitude pulse having one of N possible amplitude levels will be sent. Thus $\log_2 N$ bits of information may be conveyed by each pulse. Fig.3.3 illustrates the transmitted waveform where 4 transmission levels are used (i.e. 2 bits of information per pulse). At the receiving end of the channel, the amplitude at each clock instant is measured to determine the symbol transmitted.

Fig.3.3. Data transmission through an ideal channel (2 bits per pulse).

3.4 THE IDEAL BANDLIMITED CHANNEL: NYQUIST'S CRITERION FOR DISTORTIONLESS TRANSMISSION.

If a channel has ideal characteristics except that frequencies beyond some frequency are completely attenuated, it will not transmit a short pulse without some alteration of the waveform. As we are dealing with idealized systems, we shall overlook the fact for the time being that such a channel is not physically realizable. The response of such a channel to an impulse has the familiar (sin x)/x form:

$$h(t) = \frac{\sin 2\pi Wt}{2\pi Wt}$$

Thus if a short rectangular pulse which, if it is short enough, can be considered as an impulse, is applied to the input of an ideal bandlimited channel, the waveform at the channel output is a (sin x)/x waveform, with oscillating tails. If we just wanted to transmit a single pulse, there would be no problem, but when we transmit a succession of pulses, the tails caused by previous pulses may obscure the main response due to the pulse of the present instant. This is termed 'intersymbol interference'. Intersymbol interference can be completely avoided in the ideal bandlimited channel by sending pulses with a pulse spacing of T = W/2. That is, if the cut-off frequency of the channel is W Hz, we send 2W pulses per second. This is because h(t), the channel impulse response, is zero at t = ±W/2, ±2W/2, ±3W/2, etc. Thus, at t = nT, the channel output is solely the main lobe of the response of the channel to the nth input pulse. The response of the channel to all the other input pulses is zero at this instant, as shown in fig.3.4.

Fig.3.4. Channel response with zero intersymbol interference.

In practice it is difficult to construct bandlimiting filters giving a good approximation to the (sin x)/x impulse response and, in any case, a system using the (sin x)/x response would be sensitive to small timing errors. What is needed is a channel whose impulse response has the same property as the (sin x)/x function in being zero at t = ±W/2, ±2W/2, ±3W/2, etc., but which has a gentle roll-off with frequency. Nyquist [2] shows that if the channel gain characteristic has vestigial symmetry about a frequency equal to half the pulse transmission rate, and has a linear phase characteristic, then the impulse response of the channel has nulls at the appropriate points. A suitable response which can be closely approximated to in practice is that known as the 'raised cosine roll-off' characteristic. This is illustrated in fig.3.5. The impulse responses corresponding to various roll-off factors are shown in fig.3.6. It will be seen that the oscillations in the pulse tails decrease as the excess bandwidth is increased.

3.5 MODIFICATION OF IDEAL CHANNEL CHARACTERISTIC FOR FINITE DURATION PULSES.

In practice we shall not normally be transmitting impulses, but finite width pulses of time duration T. The desired pulse response is the same as the impulse

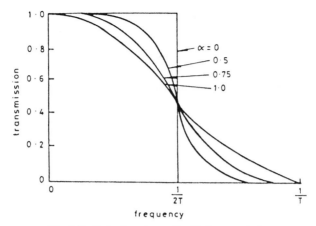

Fig.3.5 - Raised cosine roll-off characteristics.

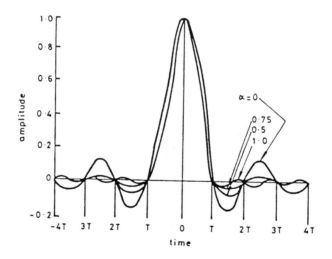

Fig.3.6 - Impulse responses of r.c.r.o characteristics.

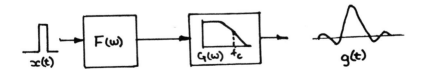

Fig.3.7 - Concept of obtaining Sin x/x response to finite pulse.

response where the vestigial symmetry of the channel occurs about a frequency 1/2T. To do this we need to modify the channel characteristic to allow for the (sin x)/x spectrum shape of the finite duration pulse. The concept is illustrated in fig.3.7.Since the spectrum for the impulse is flat, F(ω) is the inverse of the spectrum X(ω) for the pulse x(t)

$$\text{i.e.} \quad F(\omega) = \frac{1}{X(\omega)}$$

Thus, if we wish to obtain g(t) from x(t), we need to pass the signal through a channel with a gain/frequency response

$$Y(\omega) = \frac{1}{X(\omega)} \times G(\omega)$$

Since $G(\omega) = 0$ for $f > f_c + f_r$, we need not define X(ω) outside this range. In this way we can determine the channel characteristic required to give zero intersymbol interference at sampling instants spaced at intervals of T time units apart for data represented by finite-width pulses of duration T. The process is illustrated in fig.3.8.

3.6   MODULATION AND BANDPASS CHANNELS.

We have seen how it is possible to signal reliably at a limited rate through a channel whose pass-band extends from zero to some upper frequency W. Unfortunately, transmission paths encountered in the telephone network are rarely low-pass channels. Transmission bridges and a.c. coupling mean that a d.c. path is generally not available through the telecommunications network. Modulation techniques have therefore to be employed in order to shift the spectrum of the generated signal so that, instead of occupying the band from zero to WHz., it lies between f_L, the lower and f_H, the upper, edge frequencies of the channel. For low-speed data applications, frequency-shift keying (f.s.k.) is a reliable, easily implemented modulation scheme. In this scheme the binary data 0s and 1s are represented by two frequencies f_1 and f_2, respectively. Since frequency modulation produces a large number of side-bands, this modulation scheme does not make optimum use of the available bandwidth. It is not used, therefore, for high-speed data applications. The alternatives to frequency-shift keying are amplitude and phase-modulation, or a combination of both. Modulation techniques used in the telephone network are discussed in the next chapter.

3.7   BASE-BAND MODEMS

Not all data transmission involves the use of the telephone network. In many applications, especially in the local area, private wires are provided to carry data. Such circuits are normally low-pass rather than band-pass and modulation is not therefore required to translate the signal into the pass-band. However, some signal processing is usually desirable and,although the processes of modulation and demodulation are not included, it has become the custom to refer to the line terminating equipment provided to carry out this processing as a base-band modem. The base-band modem usually performs two functions. Firstly it converts the binary data input stream into a suitably encoded line signal to ensure that adequate timing information is contained in the transmitted signal and that the signal energy is sensibly distributed over the channel band-width. Some practical examples of line

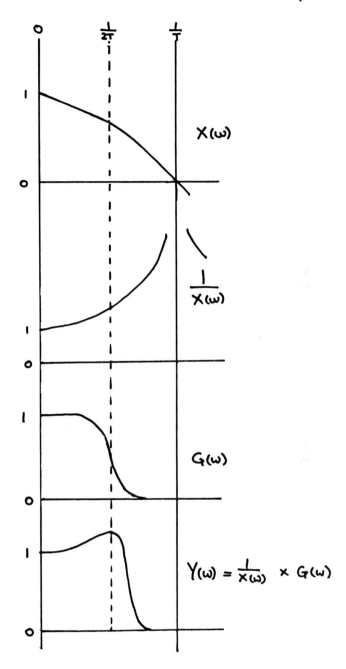

Fig.3.8 Modification of raised-cosine characteristic to allow for finite-width pulse spectrum.

codes in common use are given in chapter 6. Secondly it provides channel filtering so as to reduce the interference between adjacent transmitted pulses (intersymbol interference).

3.8   DUPLEX OPERATION

In order to obtain duplex working over a single channel, some method of separating the forward and return signals is required.   There are basically four methods that can be used.

3.8.1   Frequency Separation

The forward and return signals are modulated onto different carriers so that the two signals fall into non-overlapping frequency bands.   These can then be separated at the receivers by filtering before demodulation.   This technique is mainly used on duplex voice-band modems and the V21 modem described in the next chapter is a particular example of this technique.

3.8.2   Time Separation

The channel is used alternately to exchange groups of bits first in one direction and then in the other (Ithell and Jones [3]).   Since a guard time is required between alternate transmissions to allow for propagation along the channel, it is desirable to send bursts of bits rather than single bits in each direction.   This mode of operation is often referred to as burst mode or 'ping-pong' operation.

3.8.3   Hybrid Separation

The principle of hybrid separation has been used for many years to separate the forward and return signals in conventional telephony in order to convert from two-wire to four-wire transmission in the trunk network.   In the case of digital transmission we are less concerned with transmission loss through the hybrid and a simple Wheatstone bridge arrangement can be used.   Although the concept is basically simple, the decoupling between the forward and reverse channels is limited by the accuracy with which the input impedance of the line can be matched by the balancing network.   A digital processing structure can be used to generate inverse trans-hybrid characteristics to cancel the unwanted signal at the receiver output port. Such a device has become known as an echo-canceller (Meuller[4]).   The echo-canceller has form very similar to the transversal equalizer described later in chapter 4 and can, if necessary, be made adaptive.   Although the adaptive echo-canceller is complex, it is very effective in reducing cross-talk in duplex operation.

3.8.4   Code Separation

Coding techniques can be used in two ways to achieve duplex operation. Firstly, different line codes can be selected for each direction of transmission such that the line spectra of the two signals occupy substantially non-overlapping frequency bands in the channel.   The signals can then be separated by filtering at the receiver.   Alternatively, orthogonal codes can be used, for example codes based on the Walsh Functions, which can be separated by correlation at the receiver. Unfortunately the orthogonality of codes can be seriously affected by distortion caused by the channel characteristics, giving rise to cross-talk between the transmit and receive signals.

3.9   References

1. Shannon, C.E., 1948, 'A Mathematical Theory of Communication', BSTJ, 27, 379-423 and 623-656.

2. Nyquist, H., 1928, Certain Topics in Telegraph Transmission Theory'. Trans.AIEE., **47**, 617-744.

3. Ithell, A.H., and Jones, W.G.T., 1978, 'A proposal for the introduction of digital techniques into local distribution'. Int. Seminar on Digital Communications, Zurich.

4. Meuller, K.H., 1976, 'A new digital echo canceller for two-wire full-duplex data transmission', IEEE Trans. Comm., **24**, 956-962.

Chapter 4

Modems

J.D.Ash

4.1   INTRODUCTION

The convergence between computing and telecommunications is now an accepted fact of modern communications networks. Today's widespread application of computers for billing, information storage and retrieval, banking, word-processing, electronic mail, the "home office" and many others could not have taken place without the ability to transfer information between computers and terminals over long distances. Since its early beginnings in the 1960s, improvements in technology have enabled transfer of data to take place at higher and higher rates and with greater economy.

Over the past decade, considerable advances have been made in the introduction of digital transmission to the trunk and junction telecommunication network in the UK but, so far, its penetration into the local network has been limited. As far as the telephone user is concerned, the only available widespread network for carrying data has been, until recently, the existing analogue telephone circuits. And, in spite of the introduction of special digital data networks (such as packet switching and circuit switched digital services), this is likely to remain the most readily accessible medium for some time to come.

Unfortunately, the telephone network was designed with speech only signals in mind and little regard was paid to the problems of phase and amplitude variation with frequency, which severely limits the performance of data transmission. In addition, the presence of ac-coupled transmission bridges and the use of channel shaping filters in the trunk network excludes a dc path and effectively limits the useful frequency band to 300-3000Hz. Such a medium is unsuited to the direct transmission of digital signals, whose characteristics consist of series of rectangular pulses, producing spectral components from dc to several hundreds of kilohertz . An example of the sort of distortion which might be encountered is illustrated for a worst case pstn connection in Fig 4.1. The translation of digital signals into a form more suited to voiceband transmission is performed by a *MODEM*.

The primary purpose of a modem is to provide the means for transmitting and receiving data signals in an analogue environment but it is important to recognize that other functions are necessary to provide a "black box" approach to network connectivity (Fig 4.2).

A more detailed arrangement of the modulator and demodulator functions for a typical modem is illustrated in Fig 4.3 and discussed later in the text.

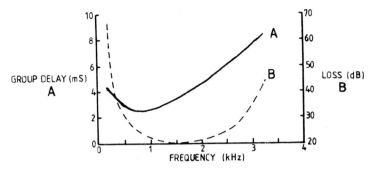

Fig 4.1 - Representative worst case PSTN connection

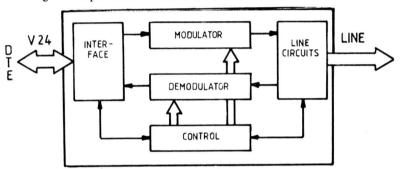

Fig 4.2 - The modem as a "black box"

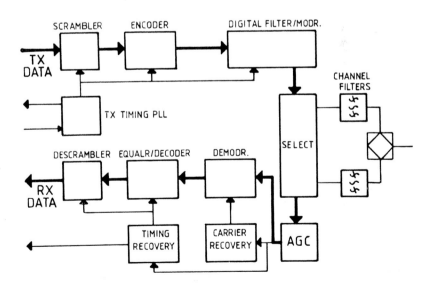

Fig 4.3 - A typical modulation/demodulation process for a half duplex
synchronous modem

4.2   MODEM TYPES

Voiceband modems generally fall into categories governed by their user bit rates, these being 300, (600), 1200, 2400, 4800, 9600 and, more recently, 14400 and 19200 bit/s.

Although 600 bit/s is seldom used nowadays, it will be noticed that all of the higher bit rates are multiples of this basic rate. In fact, this sequence is virtually an historic representation of the evolution of modems, as the technology for higher bit rates came along. Each of these speeds has one or more associated CCITT Recommendations [1], defining not only the modulation scheme employed but also the key parameters necessary to ensure compatibility across different manufacturers and across national and international boundaries. A summary of this grouping, although not exhaustive, is given in Table 4.1. In addition to the V-series recommendations listed there, it is perhaps worth mentioning three others of significance, at this stage:

V24	Defines the function of the various data and control interchange circuits, which operate across the modem/terminal interface.
V25	Defines the operation of the automatic answering and parallel interface automatic calling modems.
V25bis	Defines the operation of automatic answering and serial interface automatic calling modems.

TABLE 4.1   Common CCITT modem recommendations

CCITT Rec	Speed bit/s	Modulation	Comments
V21 (FDM)	300	FSK	2-wire duplex
V22 (FDM)	1200	PSK	2-wire duplex
V22bis (FDM)	2400	QAM	2-wire duplex
V23	1200/75	FSK	2-wire duplex (1200/75) half-duplex (1200/1200)
V26,V26bis	2400	PSK	half-duplex
V26ter	2400	PSK	2-wire duplex (echo canc.)
V27,bis,ter	4800	PSK	half-duplex
V29	9600	QAM	half duplex
V32	9600	QAM	2-wire duplex (echo canc.)
V33	14400	QAM	4-wire leased

The term "bit rate" refers to the rate at which each binary digit (bit), having the value 1 or 0, is transferred across the user interface. This should not be confused with the term "baud" (in symbols per second), which is used to express the signalling rate over the data channel itself.

A further area of delineation in modem terminology is the distinction between SYNCHRONOUS and ASYNCHRONOUS modems. An asynchronous modem conveys no timing information across the data channel, the data itself being formatted using start/stop elements. In the case of synchronous operation, the modem transmits timing information along with the data, such that each element of the data or the transmitted line signal is synchronized with a master clock. Not only is the latter more efficient, it is a prerequisite of the more complex modulation techniques employed at the higher bit rates above 1200bit/s.

4.3   MODULATION METHODS

4.3.1   Line Coding (Baseband) Techniques

We have already seen, in Chapter 3, that the effects of group delay and amplitude variations encountered on telephone circuits cause severe distortion of rectangular data pulses, to the extent that detection and restoration of the original pulse train can become impossible.

For relatively short distances, for example over copper in the local network, so called baseband or line coding techniques can be used to give reliable pulse transmission. This usually involves modifying the original unipolar pulse train from the DTE by an encoding process which converts it into a form, having more useful transmission properties. In particular, the coding would seek to eliminate the dc and the low frequency components of the original pulse train and to maximize the number of element transitions to assist timing recovery. A number of codes have been variously adopted for specific applications - some of these, such as AMI and Miller codes will be discussed in Chapter 6. In many cases, advantage is also taken of introducing additional shaping of the pulse (for example, concentrating the signal energy towards the higher frequencies can compensate for increasing line attenuation), by either predistorting the pulse with appropriate filters or by operating directly on its spectral distribution by the encoding process itself, as in the case of the once popular WAL2 code.

Baseband coding technique are used extensively in the comparatively low cost short-haul modems, for communicating across cities, where the maximum distances are in the range 10 to 20km, and where a conventional modem could be prohibitively expensive at higher bit rates. More recently, attention has been given to digital coding, in the local network, for PSS and ISDN access. In the latter case, this has led to the development of codes for use at 144kbit/s - providing two wire access to the ISDN using echo canceling techniques. (See 4.9.2)

For greater distances, extending beyond the local network and into the junction and trunk circuits, data transmission becomes more difficult, due to the line distortion referred to earlier and to the effects of phase and frequency modulation in the network. Because of this, it is necessary to translate the original digital baseband signal into the usable portion of the telephone channel, by causing it to modulate a carrier frequency, centred conveniently within the voiceband frequency range. The resulting line signal, s(t), can be expressed by

$$s(t) = A(t) \sin\{2 \int_0^t f(T)d(T) + \phi(t)\} \quad \dots \dots \dots (4.1)$$

Thus, we may choose to cause the incoming data signal to vary one (or more) of the amplitude , A, the frequency , f, or the phase , ϕ, in the modulation process. A pictorial illustration of these three approaches is shown in Fig 4.4.

4.3.2   Frequency Modulation

One of the simplest modulation methods is Frequency Shift Keying (FSK), where each binary 1 or 0 is represented by one of a pair of tones; each tone corresponding to one or other of the input binary digits. For very low bit rates, we may imagine the two tones to approximate to two corresponding spectral lines but, as the bit rate increases, the spectrum of a random data sequence spreads either side of their mean frequency.

Amplitude Modulation (2-level)

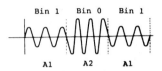

Frequency Shift Keying (FSK)

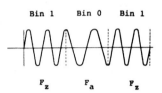

Phase Modulation (PSK)

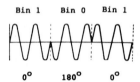

Fig 4.4 - Representation of Amplitude, Frequency and Phase modulation.

For a given bit rate, FSK signals occupy a wider bandwidth than other modulation schemes but it does have the advantage of a constant power level and a better signal to noise ratio (SNR) performance. Both generation and detection of FSK signals are relatively simple, which, in part, explains the early choice of FSK for modems up to 1200bit/s. Today, modern technology has leant itself to low price LSI realization of both V21 and V23 modems and their Bell (USA) equivalents - often all combined onto a single chip.

Table 4.2   Characteristic frequencies for CCITT Modem V23

SPEED (bit/s)	F_z (Hz) {Bin 1}	F_a (Hz) {Bin 0}
600	1300	1700
1200	1300	2100

4.3.3   Amplitude Modulation

In Fig 4.5, the carrier frequency, f_c , is directly modulated by the baseband data signal, f_m . The resultant amplitude modulated (AM) signal has both an upper and lower sideband, each of which contains identical information, together with the original carrier component.

Because the two sideband signal are identical, an improvement in bandwidth efficiency can be effected by transmitting only one of these sidebands but at the expense of introducing additional filtering circuitry into the modem. Furthermore, because the the carrier itself contains no useful information, that too may be eliminated and the available transmitter power concentrated in the one remaining sideband, with a consequential, comparative improvement in SNR performance. (In practice, a pilot carrier is usually transmitted at a reduced level, to facilitate carrier recovery at the receiving modem.) This results in a Single SideBand Suppressed Carrier system.

Reference to Fig 4.5a indicates that the baseband signal contains significant dc and low frequency energy which translates about the carrier frequency in Fig 4.5b, which must not be lost in the filtering process. Since this would place an impossible condition on the filter realization, the solution is to use a filter having a gentler roll-off about the carrier (Fig 4.5c). The symmetrical shape of the filter in the transition region allows a vestige of the upper sideband to appear, as well as the wanted sideband - thus what is "lost" from the wanted sideband is "replaced" by the vestige of the unwanted sideband. This form of modulation is called Amplitude Modulated Vestigial SideBand (AMVSB) and enjoyed some popularity in the early 1970s at 4800bit/s but later gave way to more bandwidth efficient modulation schemes.

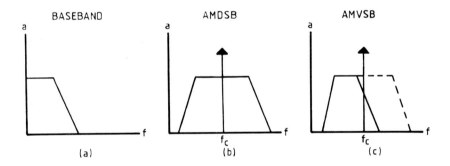

Fig 4.5 - Amplitude Modulation spectra

4.3.4   Phase Modulation

A more commonly used modulation scheme is Phase Shift Keying (PSK), in which the data elements are used to change the phase of a carrier, f_c , by a fixed amount (say, $0°$ or $180°$), corresponding to binary 1 or 0 . At the receiver, a derived reference carrier is used to decode the absolute phase values directly.

Although this form of (coherent) detection offers a theoretically optimum performance, it is easily perturbed in practice, leading to problems of phase ambiguity in the detection process. It is more usual, therefore, for each data element to be transmitted as a corresponding phase change relative to that of the preceding element; at the receiver, decoding is then accomplished by determining the relative phase change of consecutive samples of the received line signal. This Differential Phase Shift Keying (DPSK) does, however, result in a reduction in over all SNR performance, compared to coherent detection, although this can be improved, in practice, by deriving a local reference carrier in the receiver and differentially decoding the successive phase changes against it directly.

4.4   MULTILEVEL CODING

According to Shannon's classic formula [3], the information carrying capacity C, (bit/s), for a continuous channel of band width B (Hz) is given by

$$C = B\log_2 (1+S) \qquad \ldots \ldots \ldots \ldots \ldots (4.2)$$

where S is the signal to noise ratio (SNR), for white gaussian noise. Applying values to a representative telephone channel of bandwidth 2700Hz and 30dB SNR, this gives a a theoretical value for C of 27kbit/s, for the case of an ideal distortionless channel.

However, if the same values are applied to Nyquist's criterion [4] for eliminating intersymbol interference in an ideal bandlimited channel, then the theoretical maximum bit rate is given by

$$b = 2B \text{ bit/s} \qquad \ldots \ldots \ldots \ldots \ldots \ldots \ldots \ldots \ldots \ldots \ldots (4.3)$$

yielding b=5400bit/s, a figure substantially lower than Shannon's channel capacity. The double sideband spectrum of a DPSK system, such as described in 4.3.4, above, reduces the available bandwidth by half, apparently limiting data transmission to 2700bit/s maximum.

In practice, the data rate can be taken beyond this figure, by increasing the number of states which the carrier frequency f c can adopt. For example, if two data bits at a time are encoded, then the four resultant dibit (two bit) combinations (00, 01, 10, 11) would need to be represented by one of four possible carrier states. But, because each dibit pair can occupy twice the time period of the individual bit periods, the modulation rate becomes half the original bit rate. In the general case, if n bits at a time are encoded, we require 2 n possible carrier states, or in Nyquist terms

$$b = 2nB \text{ bit/s}. \qquad \ldots \ldots \ldots \ldots \ldots \ldots \ldots \ldots \ldots (4.4)$$

The penalty that must be paid for this increase in bandwidth utilization is that, not only will the modem detector need to be more complicated, there will also be a degradation in the SNR performance in going from 2 to n states. (For example, comparing 2-state 2400bit/s operation with 4-state 4800bit/s in the same bandwidth, results in a reduction in the SNR margin of approximately 6dB. In spite of this, rates of 9600bit/s are quite normal over telephone circuits and reasonable operation has been achieved at up to 19200bit/s.

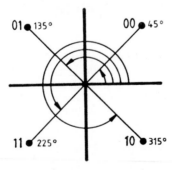

Fig 4.6 - 4-phase DPSK, corresponding to CCITT Recommendation V26bis (Alternative B)

4.4.1 Multilevel DPSK

An example of multilevel coding for a 4-state DPSK scheme is illustrated in Fig 4.6, in which two binary elements are coded for each phase state. This scheme is employed for 2400bit/s in CCITT Recommendation V26 and is extended to an eight-phase (3 bits per state) arrangement for 4800bit/s in Recommendation V27. The corresponding line signalling rates are 1200 and 1600 bauds for the two recommendations, respectively.

4.4.1.1 Gray coding. The example in Fig 4 .6 also illustrates the principle of Gray coding, by which a pair of bits (or dibits) corresponding to adjacent phase positions are made to differ by one bit only. Thus, if a given transmitted signal element, representing a particular dibit, is perturbed and incorrectly interpreted at the receiver as its immediate neighbour (say, due to "noisy" line conditions), then only one bit of the dibit pair will be decoded in error. The principle can be extended to any group of bits (be they dibits, tribits, quadbits etc). This is illustrated for the case above in Table 4.3.

Table 4.3 Gray coded dibits

Input dibit	Gray coded dibit
00	00
01	01
10	11
11	10

4.4.2 Quadrature Amplitude Modulation

In principle, one might extend the above DPSK approach still further to 16 points (equivalent to 9600 bit/s but, for each such increase, the margin against noise and phase impairments becomes progressively less. However, further improvements in bandwidth efficiency can be made, by exploiting the fact that DPSK modulation can be represented by two separate baseband signals, transmitted independently on a single carrier having the same frequency but with a 90° phase difference. This would be equivalent to simultaneously transmitting information, independently modulated by the In-phase and Quadrature components of the same carrier f_c, to produce a composite line signal. Decoding is effected by separately demodulating each channel with the appropriate in phase and quadrature components of the recovered carrier.

In the simplified arrangement of Fig 4.7, an incoming bit stream is divided into two separate streams and each applied to the I and Q channels, as described above. The resulting Quadrature Amplitude Modulated (QAM) signal constellation is illustrated in Figs 4.8 and 4.9, for different 16 point constellations. By inspection, it can be seen that each of the 16 points can be translated into one of four values on each of the I and Q axes.

The tolerance to error is determined by the proximity of one point in the constellation to its nearest neighbours and various proposals have been suggested to optimize the geometrical structure with regard to optimizing the performance for gaussian noise, phase jitter, phase/amplitude hits, differential encoding, peak/mean power, ease of implementation and so on.

Once again, however, the penalty which must be paid for this increase in bandwidth efficiency manifests itself as an increase in modem detection complexity. Perturbations in the received line signal will cause errors in both the I and Q channels; that is, each encoded channel will contain cross interference from its quadrature channel. Thus, in addition to an adaptive equalizer (see 4.7), which would normally be found in each individual channel, two additional cross-coupled equalizers are required to remove the cross channel interference. Nowadays, such an arrangement is well within the scope of modern digital signal processors and/or LSI, whereas ten years ago the implementation would have been prohibitively expensive, in terms of both component complexity and power dissipation.

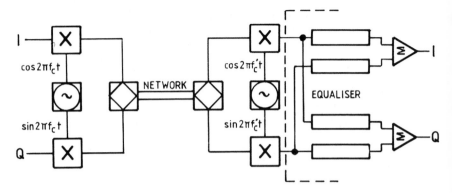

Fig 4.7 - A simplified QAM system

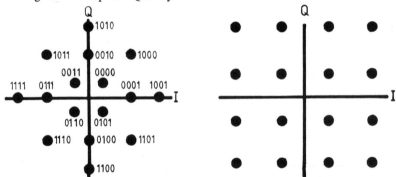

Fig 4.8 - V29 signal
space diagram

Fig 4.9 - V32 signal space diagram
(without trellis coding)

4.5 LINE SIGNAL CODING

Although modems have been produced employing larger numbers of points in the signal constellation, it carries with it the need for increasingly complex detection scheme, capable of achieving the expected bit error rate performance under all conditions of line and circuit impairments. Various coding schemes have been developed to improve the overall error rate in data transmission systems. This might involve the inclusion of additional redundant coding bits in the data encoding process, within the modem transmitter, to permit the use of predictive decoding techniques in the receiver. That is to say, the current value of the transmitted data symbol can be made dependant upon the state of the previously transmitted data symbols or upon a combinational or convolutional encoding of the input bits used in generating the current symbol - and, possibly, both. But, because any extra bits must be transmitted in addition to the actual data, this will be at the expense of increasing the number of received signal states to be decoded. The trade-off is, therefore, between the reduction in noise margin and the improvement in received bit error rate.

Recently, attention has been given to the use of one such redundant coding scheme - multilevel trellis coding [5] - in modems, which, under poor error rate conditions, exhibits a positive improvement in overall performance. One version of this coding has been standardized for use as an option on the V32 modem, where a convolutional encoding process generates a 5 bit coding signal from each information carrying quadbit (4 bits), resulting in a 32 point, rather than the 16 point constellation, of fig 4.9. The effect of this mapping produces a coding scheme which minimizes the effects of erroneous signal encoding between successive received symbols.

In spite of the more complicated detection method required - often coupled with Viterbi maximum likelihood detection schemes [6] - worthwhile benefits are claimed, particularly over digital ADPCM channels, where quantization distortion presents a severe problem for normal voiceband modem transmission. Over more conventional linearly distorted telephone channels, the benefits are less pronounced and may not always justify the added circuit complexity. A similar trellis scheme is to be found in the recent CCITT recommendation for a 14400 bit/s modem, for use on private circuits.

Various draft proposals are currently being considered within CCITT for higher speed modems on the PSTN. One such is for a 14400bit/s modem, which would include full duplex 2-wire PSTN operation, automatic rate selection for 12000, 9600, 7200, 4800 bit/s operation and a low speed reverse (backward) channel capability. Trellis coding at 14400bit/s results in a 128 point signal constellation for this modem.

4.6   THE CHOICE OF MODULATION SCHEME

It would be tempting to tabulate the individual modulation schemes against various network parameters and then select the best scheme for a given application. Such an approach is, however, less than practical, as consideration of the choice of modulation method for a given bit rate is more likely to be influenced by the ease of implementation and by its upward or downward speed compatibility with other modems, (as in the case of V22 and V22bis modems at their common 1200 bit/s rate).

In a "green field" situation, the classical method of comparing bit error rate performance with additive gaussian noise, for different modulation and detection methods, is a tempting vehicle for analysis. However, although useful, as a yardstick, for optimizing the overall design, additive noise is one of the least onerous impairments experienced on telephone circuits. Of equal importance, is the ability of both the modulation scheme and the modem itself to recover from the transient effects of impulsive noise, phase hits, phase jitter, amplitude jumps and line drop outs.

Within these confines, the CCITT sets out to agree an acceptable compromise. Note that the CCITT Recommendations are literally recommendations; in themselves they are not mandatory requirements and are restricted only to those aspects of the implementation necessary to ensure compatibility across different manufacturer's products. (Individual PTTs and Administrations are, of course, at liberty to impose a mandatory interpretation within their own territories.)

Once a Recommendation is established, the performance of a particular manufacturer's modem product is generally influenced more by the designer's ability to provide, for example, jitter tracking recovery, stable AGC circuits, optimized equalizer algorithms etc., than in his scope for modifying the modulation scheme.

4.7   EQUALISATION

But what of the effects of group delay and amplitude distortion mentioned earlier? It has already been noted that this will produce intersymbol interference in the received data signal. To a first order approximation, this could be eliminated by placing an artificial network or equalizer, having the exact inverse characteristics of the telephone channel, in the modem receiver. In practice, however, each telephone connection will have a different set of channel characteristics, requiring an infinite number of equalizer characteristics to be compensated. On some modems, attempts to approximate this approach have been made, by providing one or more manually selectable equalizers, to effect some form of Compromise Equalization - this arrangement was favoured for use on private circuit connections, where the overall network characteristics are better controlled and where the connection, once established, is seldom changed.

Where this approach is not acceptable, (and this applies to almost all medium and high speed PSTN modems), the solution is provided by the use of an Automatic or Adaptive Equalizer, which automatically adjusts itself to the network characteristics, and, in addition, compensates for the effects of echoes (delayed facsimiles of the received signal arising from reflections in the network).

A detailed exposition of adaptive equalization is beyond the scope and space limitations of this chapter (see [7] et al) but, by way of an outline description, it might take the form of the transversal filter shown in Fig 4.10. Samples of the received line signal are passed through a delay line, having a spacing at the symbol or a sub-multiple of the symbol period. By a suitable algorithm, the derived error signal can be used to add to or subtract from the pre and post distortion waveforms of successive line signals (pulses), by automatically adjusting their contribution, through control of the variable gain taps. Initial adjustment of the equalizer is achieved by transmitting a prescribed special conditioning or "training" sequence, known to the receiving modem, at the start of each transmission. The equalizer in the receiver, during this sequence, adjusts itself to minimize the effects of line distortion in the time domain; thereafter, the equalizer continually updates (or adapts) itself from the received data signal, to provide "fine tuning". In principle, this would also compensate for any time variance in the channel - although, variation in time is not usually experienced, given the relatively short duration of most data calls.

The "training" sequences are usually defined by the relevant CCITT Recommendation (V27, V29 etc) but the design parameters of the equalizer are left to the discretion of the manufacturer, who will trade performance against economy of design.

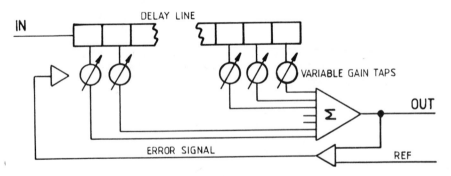

Fig 4.10 - The transversal filter as an equalizer

4.8   SCRAMBLERS

Illustrations of data signal spectra, such as that in Fig 4.5a, generally assume that the generating data sequence is of a random nature; were it not, we would see a less uniform spectrum with pronounced peaks. Not only can such peaks cause interference to adjacent channels and, potentially, other services, the lack of randomness in the data sequence prevents correct operation of the adaptive equalizer, timing and carrier recovery circuits, employed in most of the high speed synchronous modems.

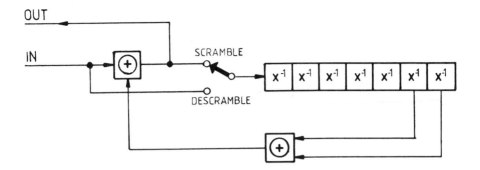

Fig 4.11 - A typical scrambler arrangement

In practice, data is seldom truly random and often contains strings of repeated patterns, which the modem randomizes by scrambling the incoming bit stream, using a shift register arrangement similar to that shown in Fig 4.11. A complementary self-synchronizing descrambler is employed in the receiver.

For compatibility reasons, the scrambling polynomials are specified by the appropriate CCITT modem Recommendation.

4.9   TWO WIRE DUPLEX MODEMS

Duplex operation - the simultaneous transmission of data in both directions - over 2-wire telephone circuits necessitates the separation of the two directions of transmission. For voiceband modems this is usually implemented in one of two accepted ways.

4.9.1   Frequency Division Multiplexing

The most obvious approach uses Frequency Division Multiplexing, in which the telephone channel is divided into two separate go and return frequency bands or channels. FDM is used for both V21 (300 bit/s) and V22 (1200 bit/s) modems to good effect but for higher speeds the problem of bandwidth limitation becomes acute; for example, the V22 bis (2400 bit/s) modem using this method requires a 16 point constellation for each channel, similar to that shown for 9600 bit/s in Fig 4.9.

4.9.2   Echo Cancellation

For higher speeds, the problem of detecting the required multilevel constellations and of designing adequate channel separation filters becomes a limiting factor and FDM is replaced by Echo Canceling (EC). With this method, the full telephone bandwidth is employed for both directions of transmission and adaptive canceling circuitry is used in the receiver to cancel the interference from both its own transmitter and its return echoes, from the network. A system of automatic and adaptive echo canceling is used, in much the same way as for the adaptive equalizers, above.

Echo cancellation in modems has received most recent exposure through the 9600 bit/s V32 recommendations but a V26ter echo canceller for 2400 bit/s DPSK (V26) was implemented by some manufacturers, although it has received less support than the alternative V22 bis FDM recommendation (due mainly to the convenience of the latter's commonality with V22).

4.10   FILTERING

If one were to look at some of the earlier modem designs, much of the hardware would be seen to consist of analogue filters. These would be mainly line and baseband filters, associated with the modem transmit and receive functions, but would also include filters for other functions, such as in the timing and carrier recovery circuits (see Fig 4.3).

In Chapter 3, reference was made to the need for pulse shaping and a raised cosine response was shown to be a realistic requirement for the overall channel shaping. By applying the concept of matched filtering, [9] et al , the necessary shaping (or filtering) should be split equally between the modem transmitter and receiver circuitry. (The theory of detecting signals in the presence of gaussian noise is beyond the scope of this chapter but see, for example, [8] & [9]).

In addition to the pulse shaping, the transmitter filter will also be needed to attenuate any unwanted higher order modulation products, whilst the receiver filters will provide immunity to other unwanted out of band signals, which might appear on the network. Often, the opportunity is also taken of including a degree of pre-emphasis or de-emphasis shaping of the transmitted and/or receive spectrum, as a form of compensation for channel distortion (see 4.7, above).

In the earlier modems, these filters would appear as complex passive or active analogue implementations but, today, most of the shaping and filtering in both the transmitter and receiver uses digital filtering as part of the digital signal processing function for both modulation and detection.

4.11   DATA CODING AND ERROR CORRECTION

With any modem, there is a high probability of errors occurring in the received data, because of both long term noise levels on the telephone networks and from shorter periods of noise bursts. To reduce the effects of this, error detection and protection methods are introduced into the data stream itself. In its simplest form this might involve packaging the data sequence into short blocks, to each of which are added additional check or parity bits. The remote end then uses these additional bits to confirm the integrity of each received block - any discrepancy results in the receiving end requesting a retransmission of the block in error.

Variations on the parity check scheme include the use of Cyclic Redundancy Check codes, in which the incoming block of data is divided by a fixed length polynomial function, the result (or the remainder) of which is added to the information (data) carrying bits in each block. At the receiver, the complete block is passed through the same polynomial function - if there has been no error, then the remainder this time should be zero. This process can be included in either the terminal equipment or in the modem itself. An example of such a scheme is given in CCITT Rec. V.41.

The purpose of any error detection and correction scheme is to eliminate the effects of line errors. However, every additional overhead bit added to the block and/or every retransmission requested has the effect of reducing the overall data throughput. In recent years, attempts to improve the transmission efficiency have resulted in proposals for more complex coding schemes, some of which combine error detection and correction with data compression and adaptive block length coding. In this field, there are already de facto "standards" in existence and CCITT have recently agreed a recommendation (V42) for both byte and bit oriented error detection and correction protocols, whilst a V42bis recommendation is being considered to include data compression algorithms.

Interestingly, a significant trend, of late, has been the increasing implementation of such schemes into the modem proper, rather than within the data terminal, as was once the more usual case (cf 4.13, below).

The final choice of modem, with or without the sophisticated protocols, such as described above, will depend upon the user and his application. For example, a user passing plain text messages (which has the built in redundancy of plain text !)

will require a much lower level of data integrity than a user passing secure coded financial data, where he may combine the above with data encryption.

4.12   MODEM CONTROL FUNCTIONS

The standard interface between the modem and the user's terminal, computer etc (collectively referred to as the Data Terminating Equipment or DTE) is governed by CCITT Rec. V24, which defines a series of interchange circuits covering the exchange of data, timing signals and control information. Although V24 covers a wide range of circuits to cater for various applications, the most commonly used are shown in Table 4.4.

Table 4.4   Some commonly used CCITT V24 interchange circuits

V24 Circuit	Description	Source	
		Modem	DTE
102	Signal ground/Common return	X	X
103	Transmitted data		X
104	Received data	X	
105	Request to Send (RTS)		X
106	Ready for S end (RFS)	X	
107	Data Set Ready (DSR)	X	
108/1	Connect data set to line)		X
108/2	Data Terminal Ready (DTR))		X
109	Received line signal detector	X	
113	Transmitter signal element timing (DTE source)		X
114	Transmitter signal element timing (Modem source)	X	
115	Receiver signal element timing	X	
125	Calling indicator	X	

More recently, the growth in integral card modems, for terminal and personal computer equipments, has seen the introduction of a new command structure or language, which enables the modem and DTE to communicate directly across the data transmit/receive interface circuits, for the purpose of configuration and control. Similar in concept to V25bis (see 4.12.2), the new procedures extend beyond the automatic call/answer to cover control of other facilities such as diagnostics, call status, speed changes, operating mode etc. As yet, there are no international standards for this approach, although the market is tending to polarize around a command set, which owes its origins to a USA modem manufacturer. Whether this, itself, becomes the accepted standard or whether CCITT and other Standards bodies move towards a recommendation of this type is uncertain, at present.

4.12.1 Automatic Modem Connection to Line

Originally, modems were manually connected to PSTN lines in both originate (Calling) and answer (Called) modes, by first establishing a speech path, using a telephone instrument, and then manually switching the modem to line. An early development was the provision of an Automatic Answering facility at the called modem, whereby the modem, on receipt of incoming ringing, automatically connected to line, permitting ready access to unattended bureaux and databases. Later developments allowed for the complementary feature of originating calls automatically, under DTE control, from an external unit, which receive d its call set up instructions and dialing information across a separate parallel interface, known as the V24 200-series interchange circuits. These external autocalling units were placed between the DTE and the modem and carried out all of the initial call set up routines, including dialing out to line; once the connection was established, the autocaller connected the modem to line and handed control over to the normal modem/DTE interface. The equipment involved tended to be bulky and relatively expensive and was used only in specialist applications.

With the arrival of microprocessor based control circuitry, the potential for providing greater intelligence within the modem, lent itself to the provision of both automatic answering and calling facilities in the modem, for very little additional cost. Unfortunately, the drawback of still having to provide the additional 200-series interface to the DTE still remained. Spurred by the advantage of auto-calling in many data communication applications, there emerged various schemes for processing serial control and number entry information across the existing transmit and receive data interchange circuits (CCTs 103 and 104).

4.12.2 Modem Control Using the Serial Data Interface

As these schemes proliferated, it became clear that there was a need for an international standard, from which arose the recent CCITT Rec. V25bis for "Automatic Calling and/or Answering Equipment on the GSTN using the 100-series Interchange Circuits", as first published in the CCITT "Red Book", during 1985. In addition to defining the Command and Response indications, V25bis also covers telephone number storage, abbreviated dialing, repeat call attempts and maintenance aspects. Thus, by differentiating between the periods when the data terminal "talks" to the modem for control purposes and those when the modem is in its normal mode of transferring data to line, the terminal can control what functions the modem should perform, prior to and even during normal modem operation.

4.13 DIAGNOSTIC FEATURES

Although most large data networks now provide an independent Network Management and/or Control capability, there still remains a need for a simple diagnostic facility within the modem itself, enabling the user to quickly determine whether the source of any problem is attributable to one or other of the network, modem or terminal equipment. The basic requirements are formulated in CCITT Rec. V54 and comprise, essentially, two main test loops, as shown in Fig 4.12.

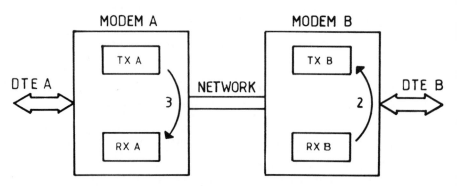

Fig 4.12 - Diagnostic features

LOOP 2   Digital Loop - loops the data received by Modem B and retransmits it for receipt and checking by Modem A

LOOP 3   Analogue Loop - loops the analogue transmit and receive signals at the local modem.

In addition to and in conjunction with these basic requirements, extra features such as internal pattern generation and checking, addressing and status monitoring are often included by the manufacturer. These facilities lend themselves to control and interrogation by the terminal, using a serial interface, similar to that described in 4.12.2, above.

4.14   LINE INTERFACING

It would be inappropriate to conclude a paper on modems without a passing reference to the line interface circuitry, which provides not only a convenient means of matching the modem to the telephone network but also affords the essential electrical safety barrier between the network and the modem (and vice versa), required by most PTTs or national administrations.

In the UK, control of these requirements has passed from British Telecom to the DTI, in the form of BS specifications, relating to both safety and network protection. At present, all modems (along with other network attachments) must be submitted for testing through the British Approvals Board for Telecommunications (BABT), before approval can be gained for connection to networks licensed in accordance with the prevailing Telecommunications Act.

It is perhaps worth noting that, within Europe, a process is in place to establish a series of standards or NETs (Normes Europeenes de Telecommunications), covering both safety and performance requirements. These standards are being formulated with the objective of enabling a common set of product approval criteria, which would be recognized across all member countries.

4.15   MODEMS - THE FUTURE

The past few years have seen fundamental changes in the evolution of modems. The bulky stand-alone modem has given way to enclosures more appropriate to the new office environment, in both style and operation, with an increasing trend towards the "board" or "chip" modem, for integration into the terminal itself. More recently, the original business market for modems has been added to by the growing use of modems by private users. This follows the trend in the entry of personal computers (PCs) into the home environment; in fact, most PC manufacturers now offer "state of the art" integral or stand-alone modems for both business and domestic applications.

Microprocessors have enabled the modem manufacturer to include intelligent control features, such as those discussed in 4.12, at little extra cost, whilst other features such as in-built error correction (fast becoming an essential selling point), data encryption, speed recognition and user configurable software are now appearing as standard. Surprisingly, through the use of new component and manufacturing technologies, all this has been achieved on a product which has seen its selling price decrease by anything up to 70% of its price ten years ago, in constant value terms.

Fifteen or twenty years ago, even the simplest modem was realized almost entirely from discrete analogue circuitry, performing the functions of modulation and demodulation, with possibly a small measure of digital integrated circuits for the final decoding and control. By the late 1970s, much of this analogue circuitry had given way to an increasing amount of digital circuitry and, by the early 1980s, the higher speed microprocessors and purpose built digital signal processors (DSPs) were finding their way into the more complex, higher speed modems, to cover virtually all the modulation, demodulation, filtering, equalization, etc.

For speeds up to the 2400bit/s duplex modem (V22bis), the "modem on a chip" is already established, for just a few pounds sterling, and the heart of the higher speed modems can be built from purpose designed DSP circuits collected together on $100cm^2$, or so, of printed circuit board. Like so many other areas of the electronics industry, this has led to semiconductor manufacturers having a direct involvement in the design and evolution of modem technology and to an increasing number of "new" modem manufacturers entering the market, who simply package these "chips" for their latest product offering.

How much further this trend will continue is difficult to predict and much will depend on the speed of transition to the all-digital ISDN networks. Already semiconductor manufacturers are producing sets of integrated circuits, which can provide all of the functions of an echo-canceling, digital transmission system, together with most of the necessary control, multiplexing, signalling and interface circuits for 144kbit/s ISDN access. Once problems of physical packaging, safety and cost have been resolved, the digital "modem" could provide the single access module between the customer's terminal (telephone, DTE, PC etc.) and the digital network.

Not withstanding all of this, whilst the nature of the product may continue to evolve, it would be premature to dismiss the traditional analogue modem this side of the 21st century.

REFERENCES

1.   International Telecommunications Union, "Data Communication Over the Telephone Network - Recommendations of the V Series", CCITT Red Book, VIII.I.

2.   Duc, N.Q., and Smith, B.M., 1977, "Line Coding for Digital Data Transmission", Aust. Telecom Rev., II, 14-27.

3.   Shannon, G.E., 1948, "A Mathematical Theory of Communication", BSTJ, 27.

4.   Nyquist, H., 1928, "Certain Topics in Telegraph Transmission Theory", Trans AIEE, 47

5.   Ungerboeck, G., 1982, "Channel Coding with Multilevel Phase Signals", IEEE Trans. Info. Theory, IT-28 No.1.

6.   Forney, G.D., 1973, "The Viterbi Algorithm", Proc. IEEE, 61.

7.   Lucky, R.W., Salz, J., and Weldon, E.J., 1968, "Principles of Data Communication", McGraw-Hill.

8.   Clark, A.P., 1976, "Principles of Digital Data Transmission", Pentech Press.

9.   Bennett, W.R., Davey, J.R., 1965, "Data Transmission", McGraw-Hill.

Chapter 5

The Philosophy of the ISO Seven-Layer Model

B.G. West and P.G. Wright

5.1 BACKGROUND

In the early 1970's it was becoming increasingly clear that computer communications were in a mess. Virtually every new device appearing on the market brought its own set of protocols with it, and simply supporting remote terminals was a major technological feat. In order to rationalize development effort, IBM produced SNA (initially Single Network Architecture, later amended to Systems Network Architecture) in 1974, the first real network architecture. The first release did not, in fact, support networking, merely communication between remote terminals and a host processor. However, it did present many of the features central to later network architectures:

*   The communications process was divided up into discrete functional layers, whose function and place in the processing hierarchy were defined by a protocol reference model.

*   Each layer provided services to the layer above and used the services of the lower layers to provide communication to its peer layer.

*   End users (terminals, applications programs, printers, etc.) were outside the scope of the architecture. They pass data to the highest layer for transportation across the network.

Gradually SNA was implemented across the range of IBM products, and was increased in functionality, flexibility, and complexity. Other manufacturers, recognizing a good thing, implemented their own (incompatible) network architectures, such as DEC's DNA.
This multitude of new networking architectures solved the problems of communications between like manufacturer's equipment, but was of no help if it was required to link equipment from different manufacturers. Some manufacturers did produce software for their equipment to support other's protocols, usually SNA, but this was by no means always the case. Thus users who required computer networks were virtually compelled to purchase their equipment from a single manufacturer.
Recognizing this problem, the International Standards Organization (ISO) started a programme to define a 'neutral' network architecture in 1978. The intention was to create an architecture which allowed the interconnection of a wide range of systems, and so was termed Open Systems Interconnection (OSI). This was greeted with mixed reactions - some manufacturers rapidly announced they would support

OSI, whilst others were less enthusiastic. Likewise, users were not universally convinced of its value, although OSI is now gaining in popularity. The first standard to emerge was the ISO 7 layer model (Ref.1), which only provides the framework for protocol definitions. Standards for the lower layer protocols have been agreed; many of these were based on existing protocols. ISO provide a choice of protocols in these layers. Standards for the highest layers are now beginning to appear, although there remains much work to be done.

5.2   The Seven Layer Model

Communications protocols are the sets of rules that govern the exchange of information in communications networks. These rules may be very complex, covering matters as diverse as the transmission of data over the physical medium (cable, radio, optical fibre), modulation, coding, multiplexing, error detection and correction, routing of messages through networks, the representation of data, etc.. As with designing a complex piece of software (which is indeed what many protocol implementations are), it is much simpler if the problem can be broken down into a number of simpler pieces. In protocols, these pieces are called layers. The key is to define all the functions a protocol has to perform and to group a few logically related functions into each layer. The reason for the term 'layer' is that these functions are arranged in a hierarchical manner, where we start with low layer functions, such as data transmission, and build upon these by adding features such as error detection and correction, routing, data translation, etc.. ISO have identified 7 logical groups of functions for a complete communication network, and hence the ISO OSI 7 layer model, illustrated in fig.5.1.

The lowest layer (Layer 1) is called the Physical layer, and as its name suggests its function is to handle physical aspects of a communications link, such as electrical characteristics, modulation schemes etc.. It provides a 'raw' data transfer service to higher layers.

Layer 2 is known a the data link layer and its function is to supplement the raw data transfer service of layer 1 by adding features such as error detection (and possibly correction), handling data in blocks (or packets or messages), maintenance of data sequencing, flow control etc.. It provides a robust data transfer service to higher layers.

Layer 3 is the network layer. Its main function is to provide addressing features which enable a message to be directed across a network, or interconnected networks, to a specified location. This and the lower layers operate on a point-to-point basis, and so a relay between two networks operates up to the network level (as also shown on fig.5.1).

Layer 4 is the transport layer, and it provides an end-to-end message transport system across the network(s). It may add further error protection etc. to provide a specified quality of service, if the lower layers are inadequate. Thus the lower 4 layers provide a complete communications service. The upper 3 layers are concerned with applications-oriented matters.

Layer 5 is the session layer, whose function is to establish a communications 'session' between applications. It may negotiate the type of interaction to be used (two way simultaneous, two way alternate, or one way) and may also provide a data 'quarantining' service where data is held until it is released by explicit command from the source, or purged.

Layer 6 is the presentation layer. This is concerned with the way in which data is represented - e.g. - ASCII or EBCDIC representation of characters at the simpler level, or abstract data structures such as databases on the complex level. The presentation layer negotiates with its peer on the form of data representation to be used; if both applications use the same representation then there is no problem, but if not, both presentation layers may transform data into some agreed representation used across the communications link.

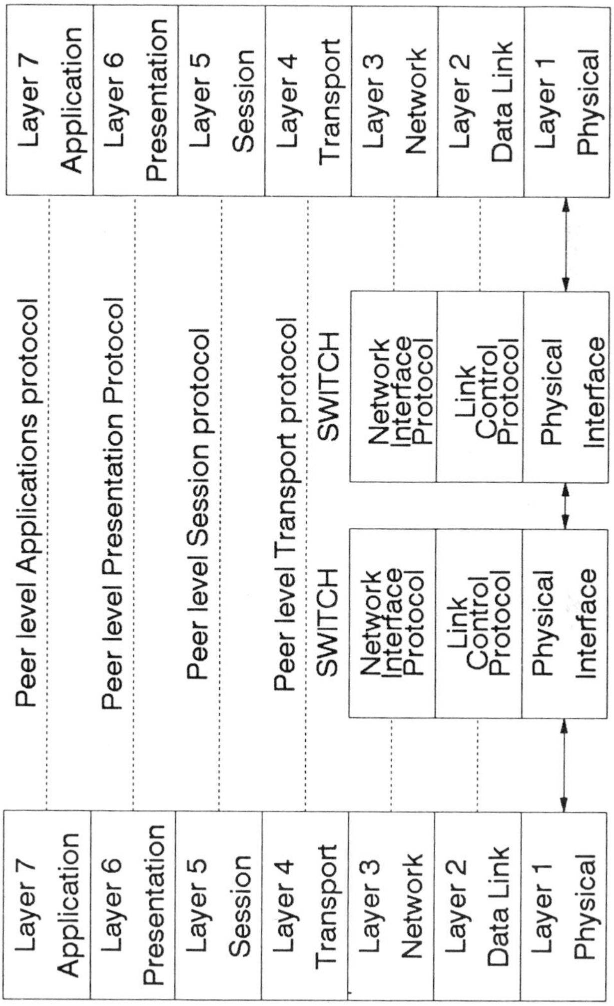

Layer 7 Application	Layer 6 Presentation	Layer 5 Session	Layer 4 Transport	Layer 3 Network	Layer 2 Data Link	Layer 1 Physical

Peer level Applications protocol

Peer level Presentation Protocol

Peer level Session protocol

Peer level Transport protocol

SWITCH

Network Interface Protocol	Link Control Protocol	Physical Interface

SWITCH

Network Interface Protocol	Link Control Protocol	Physical Interface

Layer 7 Application	Layer 6 Presentation	Layer 5 Session	Layer 4 Transport	Layer 3 Network	Layer 2 Data Link	Layer 1 Physical

Fig 5.1 : ISO OSI Protocol Reference Model

Finally, layer 7 is the applications layer. This provides the interface between the network and the application using it, which may be a user terminal, a piece of software running on a computer, a printer, a file store, etc.. There is a slightly fuzzy boundary between the actual application, outside the 7-layer model, and the services provided by the application layer, but common services such as file transfer and virtual terminal support are usually viewed as part of the application layer.

5.3 Layer Interfaces

An important aspect of layering is that the interface between two layers should be well-defined. This allows each layer to be developed independently, provided its interfaces are unchanged. Thus advances in technology can be incorporated by simply changing the affected layer - e.g.- substituting an optical network at the physical layer in place of a cable network.

The interface between two protocol layers is described in terms of Service Access Points (SAPs) and Primitives. A Service Access Point is a point at which a layer provides services to the next layer. If a layer provides a number of different services it has a SAP corresponding to each service. Primitives represent messages exchanged between two layers at a SAP. There are 4 types of Primitives, illustrated in Fig.5.2. The Request primitive is used when a higher layer requests a service from the next lower layer. This will normally result in a transaction at the lower layer with a peer layer (i.e. at the same level) elsewhere in the network, where an indication is passed up to the higher layer there. This transaction takes the form of requests down through the layers to the physical layer, a message or messages passing over the physical link, and indications passing up through the layers at the destination. The higher layer at the destination may generate a Response in reply to the Indication, and that will be passed back to the source, where a Confirmation may be passed up to the original requesting layer.

The data passed through a service access point for onward transmission is termed a Service Data Unit (SDU). The functions within the layer may add Protocol Control Information (PCI) (e.g. frame header and checksum). The SDU and PCI combined form a Protocol Data Unit (PDU), which is then passed to the next lower layer, where it becomes the SDU at that layer (see Fig.5.3). Thus as a message is passed down through the layers, it is extended as it acquires protocol information at each layer. This information is usually added to the beginning or end of a message and so is likened to adding extra 'skins'. In addition, a layer is free to rearrange messages, either dividing messages into smaller units for transmission, or combining small messages into larger blocks for efficiency, provided they are reassembled correctly at the destination, and the specified quality of service is maintained (e.g. message delay).

5.4 Connection-Oriented and Connectionless Operation

There are two major modes of operation of networks, connection-oriented or connectionless. The OSI model was originally aimed at connection-oriented operation, which is the traditional mode of operation whereby a connection is set up, a number of transactions are performed, and then the connection is terminated (e.g. telephony or login to a computer). This covers both circuit-switched networks (e.g. telephony) and virtual-circuit networks, where a physical circuit is not actually set up, but a route is established through a network and is termed a virtual circuit (e.g. X25 packet-switching). For connection-oriented mode, the upper protocol layers will certainly operate in connection-oriented mode, with a separate connection establishment phase, data transfer phase, and disconnection phase. Usually the lower layers also (at least down to the network layer) will operate in this mode, although this is not obligatory.

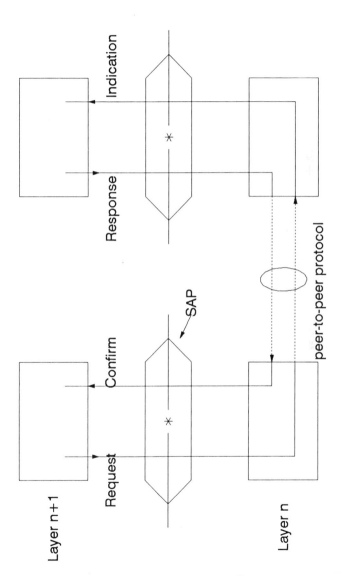

Layer n+1

Request

Confirm

SAP

Response

Indication

Layer n

peer-to-peer protocol

Fig 5.2: Service Access Points and Primitives

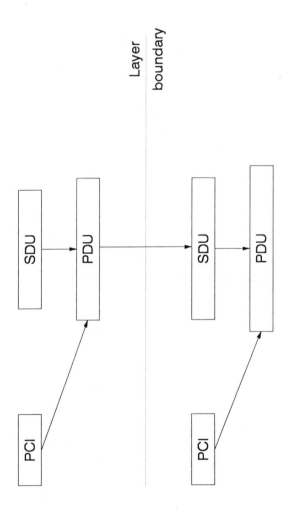

Fig 5.3 : SDU's, PCI's and PDU's

The connectionless mode of operation does not have these three phases of operation, i.e., no establishment or disconnection phases. Each block of data is sent independently, and therefore must be fully self-contained, i.e., it must carry all addressing information to enable it to be routed to its destination. It is most suited to applications requiring very few interactions, where the overhead of setting up and removing connections would be high. On the other hand, when a connection has been established the data transfer phase messages do not require addressing information and so this mode of operation is more efficient for applications involving more message transfers. Normally one would expect all layers to be connectionless, for although it is possible to operate a connectionless upper layer over a connection-oriented lower layer, it would be rather inefficient. One disadvantage of connectionless operation is that it does not necessarily maintain the order of arrival of messages; higher layers operating over a connectionless layer may have to take special actions to maintain message sequencing.

Connectionless mode operations have been added to the OSI model and protocols.

5.5 Standards Activities

Besides ISO, a number of other organizations are also working on protocol standards. These include CCITT (The International Telegraph and Telephone Consultative Committee), ECMA (The European Computer Manufacturer's Association) and the IEEE (Institute of Electrical and Electronic Engineers). Fortunately, a great deal of liaison occurs between these various groups, avoiding conflicting standards. Indeed, many standards issued by one group are adopted by others. For example, the IEEE CSMA/CD standard 802.3 has been adopted as a physical layer standard by ISO (DIS 8802/3), and the CCITT X200 series recommendations mirror ISO recommendations (see Table 5.1).

Table 5.1: Current Standards for OSI

	ISO	CCITT
Reference Model	ISO7498	X200
Network Service	ISO8348	X213
Transport Service	ISO8072	X214
Transport Protocol	ISO8073	X224
Session Service	ISO8326	X215
Session Protocol	ISO8327	X225

Government agencies are also involved in promoting OSI, for example, the DTI in the UK has produced a series of 'intercept' recommendations to encourage industry to develop products. These recommendations are based on working documents in important areas where stable standards have not yet emerged (for example the enhancement of X21 and X25 to provide a full OSI Network service). In Europe, the CEC is also involved in setting and promoting standards, via CEN/CENELEC/CEPT and now ETSI. Procurement policies are also encouraging OSI standards by requiring equipment to conform to these standards.

5.6   Implementation Issues

It may come as a surprise following the above that even if two products conform to OSI, it does not guarantee that they will interwork. The problem is that OSI only sets a framework for the protocols, but at each layer there are a number of protocols which could be selected. This has been tackled by SPAG (the Standards Promotion and Applications Group), which has selected a number of "profiles" for common types of applications. These select the appropriate protocols at each level, and resolve any optional features contained in these protocols. Thus equipment from any manufacturer conforming to a given profile should interwork.

The description of protocols as a layered   structure is not intended to constrain their implementation - although it may well be convenient to implement each layer as a software process, it is not obligatory, and layers may be combined, or split into sublayers as felt appropriate. Older protocols, which predate OSI, do not fit the layered structure precisely, although attempts are made to do so. Hardware implementations of lower layers, especially physical and data-link are increasingly becoming available.

5.7   Conclusions

The OSI standards are now gaining in popularity both with manufacturers and users. Its advantages include

*   Manufacturer independence. It is much simpler to attach dissimilar equipments to networks when using OSI standards.

*   Network independence. It is easier to change the underlying network (e.g. cable to optical fibre), by merely replacing low layer protocols, without change to any higher layers, so from the user's point of view, no change is visible (except perhaps for improved quality of service).

*   Flexibility. Use of common standards enables users to have a single point of access to a number of systems, i.e. true "openness". This facilitates both intra-company and inter-company communications, and encourages the use of information processing resources.

A number of disadvantages may be devised, but many of these are temporary or rather spurious; for example:

*   Standards are not fully stable. At present the upper layers are not fully defined, but work is proceeding, and this argument cannot be used in the future.

*   Performance. One could easily conclude that implementing all these complex protocol layers would result in poor performance. This is indeed true of purely software implementations on low-power processors, but as more functions are implemented in hardware and more powerful processors become available, this argument also loses its significance.

*   Security. The very term 'open' seems to imply a lack of security, but this is not intended. Security depends to a large extent on procedures outside the OSI environment - such as access control. There is no reason why encryption cannot be added as a function in a number of layers of the OSI model, and in fact work on these aspects is progressing.

Thus the advantages far outweigh the disadvantages, and coupled with the active promotion of OSI by government agencies and procurement policies, we see a great future for OSI.

5.8 References and Bibliography

1. "Information Processing Systems - Open Systems Interconnection-Basic Reference Model", ISO7498, International Standards Organization, Geneva, 1984.

2. Tanenbaum, A. "Computer Networks", Prentice-Hall, 1981.

3. Sloman, M. and Kramer, J. "Distributed Systems and Computer Networks", Prentice-Hall, 1987.

4. Jenkins, P.A. and Knightson, K.G., "Open Systems Interconnection - The Reference Model", British Telecom Technology Journal, Vol 2 No.4 September 1984.

5. Woodcock, A. "Towards the Application of OSI standards", Computer Networks and ISDN Systems, 14 (1987) pp 291-295.

Chapter 6

Coding

Dr Ron Brewster

6.1 INTRODUCTION

In this chapter we will be looking at four entirely different aspects of coding. Firstly we shall look at source coding, where we derive low redundancy coding schemes to represent the messages selected for transmission by the data source. This enables us to represent our transmitted information using a minimum of data symbols in our transmitted message sequence. This process is often referred to as 'coding down' as it minimizes the number of symbols required to transmit the selected message.

Secondly, we shall look at the possibilities of providing coding in order to carry out error detection and/or correction. This involves adding further 'redundant' bits to enable errors to be located in the message sequence. Redundant bits are those that do not carry actual transmitted information. Since additional bits have to be added in order to implement the error detection and/or correction code, the process is often referred to as coding up.

A message sequence consisting of randomly selected data symbols may not necessarily produce a signal which can be transmitted directly over the available communication channel. By the use of a suitable line-coding technique, it is often possible to map the symbol sequence into another sequence which does have suitable properties for direct transmission. We shall therefore consider briefly the design and implementation of a selection of line codes in common use.

Finally, it is often desirable to convert a systematic message sequence into a 'random' (properly pseudo-random) sequence of symbols before transmission. This may be simply to avoid systematic patterns producing strong frequency components in the line signal, which may cause cross-channel interference. Alternatively, it may be employed to ensure security of sensitive information during transmission.

6.2 SOURCE CODING

If messages are selected from a message set where all messages are equiprobable, then every message carries the same information and direct coding into groups of binary digits is all that is needed. However, if the messages have widely varying probabilities, then the information associated with the least probable messages is greater than that associated with the most probable messages. Since the least probable messages also occur less frequently, it is sensible that they should be associated with larger groups of binary digits than the more frequent, highly probable, messages. In this way it is possible to minimize the number of digits required to transmit a message sequence to somewhere near the actual information content of the messages. Two well-known low-redundancy source coding techniques are the Shannon-Fano and Huffman codes.

6.2.1 Shannon-Fano Encoding.

In Shannon-Fano encoding, the messages are firstly ranked in descending order of probability as shown in table 6.1.

Table 6.1   Example of Shannon-Fano code.

Source message	Probability $P(x_i)$	Code words representing each message
x_1	0.25	0 <u>0</u>
x_2	0.25	0 <u>1</u>
x_3	0.2	1 <u>0</u>
x_4	0.15	1 1 <u>0</u>
x_5	0.08	1 1 1 <u>0</u>
x_6	0.04	1 1 1 1 <u>0</u>
x_7	0.02	1 1 1 1 1 <u>0</u>
x_8	0.01	1 1 1 1 1 1

The table is then progressively subdivided into pairs of sub-sections, binary 0 being attributed to one sub-section and binary 1 to the other, until it is impossible to sub-divide further. In this way, the more probable messages have fewer binary digits than the less probable. The overall average number of bits per message for the example given is 2.55 bits/message. This is significantly less than the 3 bits/message required to transmit the data using direct binary encoding of the messages. The received bit sequence can readily be separated into the individual message groups by tasking bits until a recognized message sequence has been obtained. This is possible since the method of generating the code ensures that no code word forms the initial part of another longer code word.

6.2.2 Huffman Coding.

Huffman coding [1] produces basically similar results to the Shannon-Fano code. Again, the messages are firstly ranked in descending order of probability as shown in table 6.2. However, in this case the two least probable messages are combined and the list re-ranked. This procedure is repeated until all the message groups have been combined. At each combination point the binary symbols 0 and 1 are attributed to each sub-division. The message code words are then determined by tracing backwards through the combinatorial chain, noting the 0s and 1s passed on the way to the original ranking column. The separation of the received bit sequence into individual message groups is performed exactly as for Shannon-Fano, since the condition that no code word forms the initial part of another longer code word is also satisfied by the Huffman code.

Table 6.2.   Example of Huffman coding.

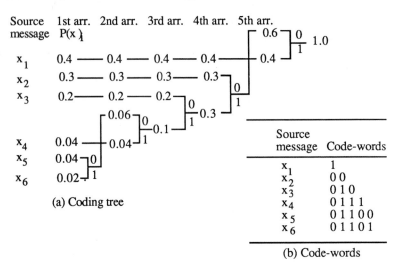

(a) Coding tree

Source message	Code-words
x_1	1
x_2	0 0
x_3	0 1 0
x_4	0 1 1 1
x_5	0 1 1 0 0
x_6	0 1 1 0 1

(b) Code-words

6.3.   ERROR DETECTING AND CORRECTING CODES

If additional bits are added to the data stream of information-bearing bits, it is often possible to detect, and even correct, at least a fair proportion of any errors that may occur in transmission. The degree to which this can be achieved depends on the proportion of extra "redundant" bits that one is prepared to allocate to this task. Obviously, the larger the proportion of the transmission capability that is used for error detection/correction purposes, the smaller the proportion that is left for transmission of actual data.   Simple error detection requires much less redundancy than is requires to provide a "forward" error correction facility.   Forward error correction implies that the errors can be corrected without further reference to the message source.   The alternative to forward error correction is correction by detection of errors and retransmission of packets found to be in error.   This method of operation is known as ARQ (automatic repeat request).

The simplest method of detection of single errors in a data packet is the addition of a single parity bit.   This bit is chosen so that there is always an even number of 1s in the message-plus-parity bit (even parity) or an odd number of 1s in the message-plus-parity bit (odd parity).   Examples of even and odd parity are given in Fig.6.1.

Block Code	Even parity
1 0 1 1 0 1 0 1	1
0 0 0 1 1 0 1 1	0

Fig.6.1 - Block parity for single error correction.

A single error in any data packet will then lead to parity violation, since either a 1 will have become a 0 or a 0 a 1, in both cases changing the parity of the message packet. Of course, double errors will go undetected, but these are much rarer than single errors. The probability of error increases with packet size. The packet size must therefore be chosen so that the number of incorrect packets accepted as correct is below some acceptable threshold. It is quite impossible to ensure that no erroneous packets are ever accepted.

By arranging the data packet into block format and employing multiple parity checks as shown in Fig.6.2, it is possible to locate the position of single errors by means of a double parity failure and, since the bit can only be in one of two states, it can be corrected by bit reversal. Again multiple errors may go undetected.

a	b	c	d	P1
e	f	g	h	P2
i	j	k	l	P3
P7	P6	P5	P4	

Fig.6.2 - Block parity for single error correction.

6.3.1 Hamming Codes

A more efficient single-error-correcting code can be implemented using a method first proposed by R.W.Hamming [2]. In the Hamming Code, parity bits are systematically introduced as shown in Fig.6.3.

The position of errors in transmission are indicated by the coding failure syndrome as shown in the figure. Because of the economical use of redundancy in the Hamming Code, unfortunately double errors are usually interpreted as single errors from a different coding group and are incorrectly "corrected" so that the double error becomes a triple error at the receiver terminal. However, by careful choice of block size it is possible to ensure that double errors occur only with a relatively small probability. Typically, a (7,4) Hamming Code (i.e. the block size is 7 bits with 4 information bits and 3 check bits) will reduce the average bit error-rate from 1 in 10^4 to about 1 in 10^7. The larger the block size the smaller the proportion of the redundancy but the lower the effectiveness of the code in overall error-correcting performance.

Data	K1	K2	Data	K3	Data		
	1	2	3	4	5	6	7
0	0	0	0	0	0	0	0
1	1	1	0	1	0	0	1
2	0	1	0	1	0	1	0
3	1	0	0	0	0	1	1
4	1	0	0	1	1	0	0
5	0	1	0	0	1	0	1
6	1	1	0	0	1	1	0
7	0	0	0	1	1	1	1
8	1	1	1	0	0	0	0
9	0	0	1	1	0	0	1
10	1	0	1	1	0	1	0
11	0	1	1	0	0	1	1
12	0	1	1	1	1	0	0
13	1	0	1	0	1	0	1
14	0	0	1	0	1	1	0
15	1	1	1	1	1	1	1

K_1 is even parity on positions 1, 3, 5, 7.
K_2 is even parity on positions 2, 3, 6, 7.
K_3 is even parity on positions 4, 5, 6, 7.
Data is given in binary form in positions 3, 5, 6, 7.
Single errors cause failure of parity checks thus:
(1 = failure, 0 = check passed)

	K3	K2	K1
No error	0	0	0
Error in position 1	0	0	1
Error in position 2	0	1	0
Error in position 3	0	1	1
Error in position 4	1	0	0
Error in position 5	1	0	1
Error in position 6	1	1	0
Error in position 7	1	1	1

Fig.6.3 - Hamming code for N = 7, n = 3

6.3.2 Cyclic Redundancy Check Codes

The codes we have discussed so far are powerful only in detecting and/or correcting single errors. This is useful where errors are randomly distributed because double errors per block then become much less probable than single errors. In many practical situations errors can occur in bursts rather than at random, due to the nature of the line impairment. The codes discussed so far are quite unable to deal with burst errors. Error detection of multiple errors can be achieved using cyclic redundancy check codes. In these codes, the code block is "divided", using Boolean arithmetic operations, to give a "remainder" which is transmitted following the information field of the packet. The nature of Boolean arithmetic means that the received packet, including the "remainder" field, should be precisely divided by the same binary divisor as used by the sender. If any of the bits are changed it is highly improbable that the received field will be precisely divisible by the divisor. A remainder will therefore indicate errors in the received message. The power of the code to deal with multiple and burst errors depends on the choice of the divisor, both in number and distribution of bits. However, even 16 bit check fields give enormous error detection power. The CRC code using the divisor 10001000000100001 used on a field of 240 bits is recommended by CCITT for a number of applications, including HDLC checking in X25. A simplified example of a CRC code is given in Fig.6.4.

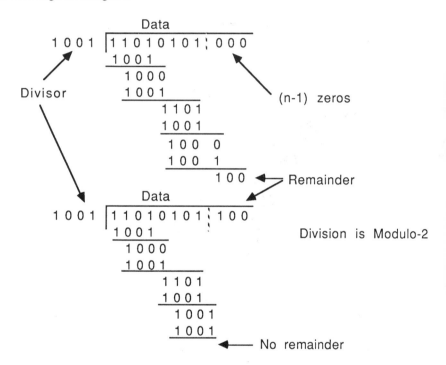

Fig.6.4 - Example of cyclic redundancy code generation.

6.3.3 Convolution Codes

For burst error correction it is necessary to interleave the correction check bits into the data stream in such a way that they are not impaired by the same burst as the data they are being used to check. This process of interleaving is referred to as convolution. There are many varieties of convolution code in use. We only have space here to consider one simple example, the Hagelbarger Code [3].

6.3.4 The Hagelbarger Code

In the Hagelbarger Code alternate bits in the transmitted data stream are check bits formed by modulo-2 sum of two separated preceding information bits.

This means that information about a single information bit is held in three places spread out in time according to the selection of the relative positions of the checked information bits. The redundancy of such a code is 50%. The Hagelbarger code is illustrated in Fig.6.5

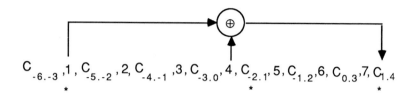

$$C_{-6.-3},1, C_{-5.-2},2, C_{-4.-1},3, C_{-3.0},4, C_{-2.1},5, C_{-1.2},6, C_{0.3},7, C_{1.4}$$

* Positions containing information relating to digit 1

Fig.6.5 - The Hagelbarger code.

In this example a parity check on the information bits in the 1st and 7th positions in the data stream is inserted at the 14th position in the stream. In this particular example up to six consecutive errors would be corrected, provided there are at least 19 error-free digits between bursts of error.

6.4   LINE CODES

The simple binary bipolar code, where 1 is represented by a positive impulse and 0 is represented by a negative impulse, and the simple unipolar code, where 1 is represented by a positive impulse and 0 is represented by no signal, both suffer from the existence of strong frequency components at low frequencies and a lack of signal transitions with long strings of 0s or 1s are transmitted. These transitions are necessary to derive timing signals for the receiver decoder. Their basic nature, however, make them a useful reference of comparison for more complex code arrangements. Two modified binary line codes are the Walsh function codes Wal 1 and Wal 2 (Duc and Smith [4]). These are illustrated in Fig.6.6(a). In both cases the line signal is free from d.c. component and contains a large number of transitions from which timing information can be recovered, whatever the transmitted data pattern. The line spectra for these two codes are shown in Fig.6.6(b). In both cases the spectrum has no d.c. component and low l.f. components. The bandwidth occupancy of the Wal 2 is slightly greater than the Wal 1, extending to approximately twice the transmission rate. The Wal 2 spectrum has no significant content below 0.2 of the transmission rate, a fact that can be made use of in data-over-voice applications. Another useful binary code is the Miller code, or delay modulation, as it is sometimes called. This code is a variation of the Wal 1 and is derived by deleting every second transition in a Wal 1 signal, as illustrated in Fig.6.6(a). The spectrum shape of the line signal is given in Fig.6.6(b), where it can be compared with Wal 1 and Wal 2 spectra. Although it has a small d.c. component, it has the advantage of a more limited band-width requirement than the comparable Wal codes.

Ternary codes operating on three signal levels, the middle level of which is usually zero volts, have found wide application as line codes. The best known of the ternary codes is Alternate Mark Inversion (AMI). The encoded sequence is obtained by representing the mark in the binary sequence alternately by positive and negative impulses whilst the spaces are represented by no signal. The AMI code has very attractive properties. The line signal power density spectrum has no d.c.

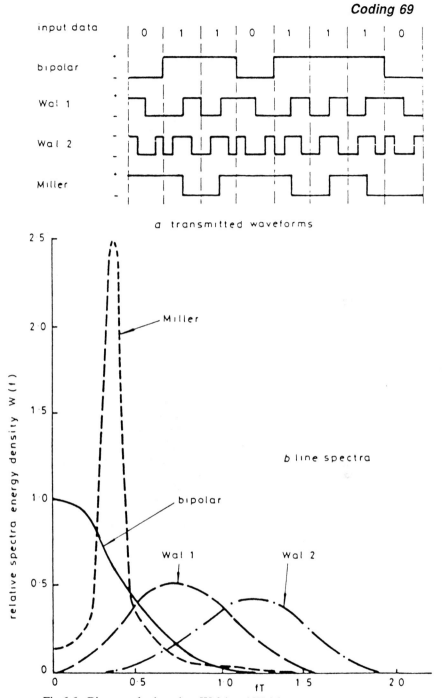

Fig.6.6 - Binary codes based on Wal 1 and Wal 2.

component and very small l.f. spectrum content. The coding and decoding circuitry requirements are quite simple and some degree of error monitoring can be achieved by simply observing violations of the AMI rule. The band-width required is equal to the transmission rate. It has the disadvantage that it has a poor timing content associated with long runs of binary zeros. There are two useful ternary codes which fall within the sub-class of linear pseudo-ternary codes (Crosier [5]). These codes are designated pseudo-ternary since they are determined by a set of rules which assign a three-level signal to a binary message and linear because the pseudo-ternary code is linearly derived directly from the binary message. A linear pseudo-ternary code is actually a particular case of a binary code in which the signal element $S_0(t)$ has been replaced by

$$S_0'(t) = S_1(t) \times S_0(t)$$

where $S_1(t)$ is the sequence of impulses

$$S_1(t) = \sum_{k=0}^{K} \alpha_k (t - kT)$$

A linear pseudo-ternary encoding is thus equivalent to a filtering operation, the frequency response being given by the Fourier transform of $S_1(t)$

$$S_1(\omega) = \sum_{k=0}^{K} \alpha_k e^{-jkT}$$

In order for the coded signal to have only three possible values for any sequence, it is necessary that there be only two $\alpha_k \neq 0$ and that they are either equal or opposite. We thus have two basic pseudo-ternary codes: the twinned binary in which $\alpha_0 = -0.5$ and $\alpha_1 = +0.5$ (or the other way round) and the duobinary code, in which $\alpha_0 = \alpha_1 = +0.5$. The AMI and pseudo-ternary codes are illustrated in Fig.6.7, together with the power spectra for random data using these codes. The duobinary code has all its energy concentrated at low frequencies and has a very strong d.c. component. However, since the significant spectrum band-width is equal to only half the data rate, the code is attractive for use in limited band-width applications. The twinned binary code band-width is equal to the transmission rate and most of the signal energy is concentrated around half the bit-rate. The code is easily generated and has an error-detecting capability since it obeys the AMI rule. The code is, however, sensitive to error in the decoding operation due to error propagation in the decoding circuit.

There are also two classes of non-linear ternary codes which have application in the field of data transmission, namely alphabetic and non-alphabetic codes. In the alphabetic codes, n binary digits are taken together as a signal element which can be regarded as a selection from an alphabet of 2^n possible characters. The character is then encoded into m ternary digits where $3^m > 2^n$. Such codes are normally described as nBmT codes. The simplest of these codes is given by n = m = 2 and is generally known as Pair Selected Ternary (PST). The message signal is grouped in 2-bit words which are then coded in ternary as given in table 6.3.

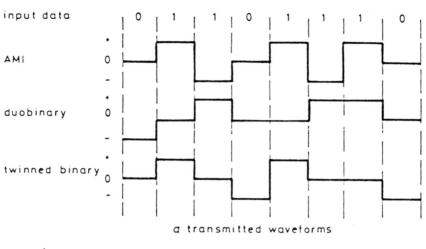

a transmitted waveforms

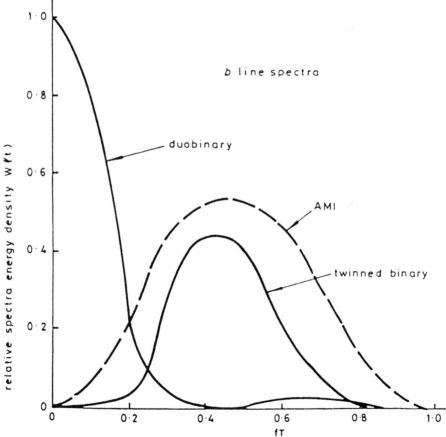

Fig.6.7 - AMI and linear pseudo-ternary codes.

Table 6.3   PST Code translation

Binary Word	Ternary Word		
	Mode A	Mode B	Word Digital Sum
0 0	- +	- +	0
0 1	0 +	0 -	±1
1 0	+ 0	- 0	±1
1 1	+ -	+ -	0

It can be seen there is no change in the rate of transmission. With this code the d.c. component is reduced by the alternating mode which is equivalent to the alternating polarity of AMI coding. Timing content is assured by the translation of pairs of zeros into alternating pulses. The mode alternation also provides some error monitoring capability. The average power spectrum is given in Fig.6.8(a). The drawbacks of the code are that it has high l.f. components and the transmission power is about 1.5 times that of AMI for similar performance.

A widely used alphabetic code is that known as 4B3T. The original binary data stream is divided into words of four bits, each word being encoded into three ternary digits, as shown in table 6.4. The average power spectrum of the 4B3T code with random data is given in Fig.6.8(a). The power is fairly evenly distributed throughout the spectral band but there is a significantly large component at the low frequency end of the spectrum. Some attempts to overcome this large l.f. content have been made by the introduction of modified 4B3T codes. Two of these are the MS-43 code and the VL-43 code. The average power spectra for these two codes are also given in Fig.6.8(a).

Table 6.4   4B3T code translation

Binary Word	Ternary Word		
	Mode A	Mode B	Word Digital Sum
0 0 0 0	+ 0 -	+ 0 -	0
0 0 0 1	- + 0	- + 0	0
0 0 1 0	0 - +	0 - +	0
0 0 1 1	+ - 0	+ - 0	0
0 1 0 0	+ + 0	- - 0	±2
0 1 0 1	0 + +	0 - -	±2
0 1 1 0	+ 0 +	- 0 -	±2
0 1 1 1	+ + +	- - -	±3
1 0 0 0	+ + -	- - +	±1
1 0 0 1	- + +	+ - -	±1
1 0 1 0	+ - +	- + -	±1
1 0 1 1	+ 0 0	- 0 0	±1
1 1 0 0	0 + 0	0 - 0	±1
1 1 0 1	0 0 +	0 0 -	±1
1 1 1 0	0 + -	0 + -	0
1 1 1 1	- 0 +	- 0 +	0

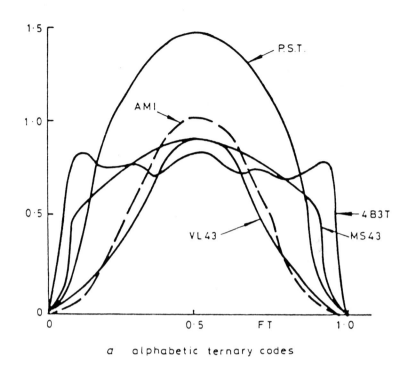

a   alphabetic ternary codes

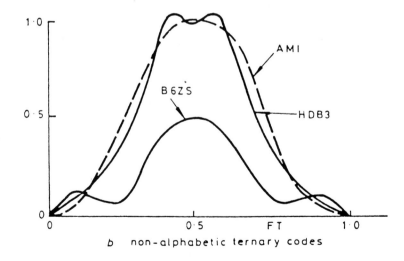

b   non-alphabetic ternary codes

Fig.6.8 - Power spectra for ternary coded random data.

In the non-alphabetic codes, long runs of zeros which may occur in conventional AMI coding are broken up by the substitution of pulses, or groups of pulses, which violate the AMI alternating mark pulse polarity rule.   There are a number of ways in which this may be carried out and the most useful of these are described in [5].   The average power spectra for the two most important non-alphabetic codes are given in Fig.6.8(b).   These are the B6ZS (Binary with Six Zeros Substitution) and the HDB3 (High Density Binary with maximum of three consecutive zeros).

Codes using more than three pulse amplitude levels are possible.   For instance, quarternary (four-level) codes can be simply derived by taking pairs of bits from the binary input sequence and converting them into pulses with amplitudes -3, -1, +1, +3 corresponding to the binary pairs 01, 00, 10 and 11 respectively.   This particular code is often referred to as 2B1Q (two binary digits into one quarternary symbol).   This procedure can be extended by taking n bits at a time and converting them into an m-ary signal, where $m = 2^n$.

Another technique using multilevel signalling is the generalized partial response coding (Kretzmer[6]).   The linear pseudo-ternary codes described earlier are the simplest forms of partial response coding.   Higher order partial response codes make use of an increasing number of amplitude levels to define the signal. The main disadvantage of the multilevel codes is that the higher number of levels makes them very vulnerable to interference from external sources such as cross-talk, impulsive noise and radio pick-up.

6.5   SCRAMBLING AND ENCRYPTION

The proper operation of data transmission equipment often depends on the fact that the data source generates the binary data symbols completely randomly.   In practice long strings of data can be generated that are anything but random.   Rest conditions can involve the transmission of long strings of binary 0s or 1s or, perhaps, 'reversals' or 'dotting' patterns consisting of alternate 0s and 1s.   It is desirable, therefore, to be able to produce random, or apparently random, strings of binary digits which may be used as test signals or for the purposes of data randomization ('scrambling').

6.5.1 Pseudo-Random Binary Sequences

The usual method of generating an apparently random binary sequence is to use a sequential feed-back shift-register arrangement which will generate a maximal length pseudo-random binary sequence (p.r.b.s.), often referred to as an 'm' sequence.

Consider an n-stage shift-register with feed-back connections via exclusive-OR gates as shown in Fig.6.9, where Ck, k = 1 to n, takes the value 0 or 1.

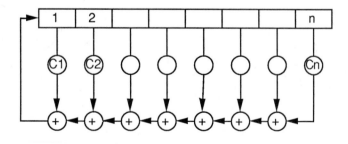

Fig.6.9 - N-stage feed-back shift-register.

By suitable choice of the values of the coefficients Ck, it is possible to make the shift-register cycle through all the possible n-tuples sequentially, except the all-zero n-tuple. If the register ever contains the all-zero n-tuple, then it will remain in this state indefinitely. The operation of the shift-register arrangement is dependent on its 'characteristic polynomial'. The characteristic polynomial is given by

$$\phi(x) = 1 + \sum_{k=1}^{n} C_k x^k$$

To obtain a maximal length sequence, the characteristic polynomial must be primitive. The powers of x in the characteristic polynomial either exist or do not exist, depending on whether the appropriate value of C is 1 or 0. Thus the powers of x that exist in the polynomial actually define the tap connections that are made in the shift-register. The characteristic polynomial is therefore often referred to as the tap polynomial. To minimize the hardware necessary to implement the m-sequence generator, it is obviously desirable to minimize the number of taps required to the shift-register. In fact, it is frequently possible to obtain a maximal-length sequence with only two tapping points, an intermediate point and the end of the shift-register. Unfortunately this cannot be done with a shift-register of length 8 and various other lengths greater than 8. These require a minimum of 4 tapping points, 3 intermediate and one at the end of the shift-register.

Table 6.5 - Characteristic polynomials for m-sequence generators.

n	polynomial	n	polynomial
3	$X^3 + X^2 + 1$	4	$X^4 + X^3 + 1$
5	$X^5 + X^3 + 1$	6	$X^6 + X^5 + 1$
7	$X^7 + X^6 + 1$	8	$X^8 + X^7 + X^2 + X + 1$
9	$X^9 + X^5 + 1$	10	$X^{10} + X^7 + 1$
11	$X^{11} + X^9 + 1$	12	$X^{12} + X^{11} + X^{10} + X^2 + 1$
13	$X^{13} + X^{12} + X^{11} + X + 1$	14	$X^{14} + X^{13} + X^{12} + X^2 + 1$
15	$X^{15} + X^{14} + 1$	16	$X^{16} + X^{14} + X^{13} + X^{11} + 1$
17	$X^{17} + X^{14} + 1$	18	$X^{18} + X^{11} + 1$
19	$X^{19} + X^{18} + X^{17} + X^{14} + 1$	20	$X^{20} + X^{17} + 1$

Suitable characteristic polynomials for shift-registers from length 3 to 20 are given in Table 6.5. These are not the only primitive polynomials for each length of shift-register but they do make use of the minimum possible number of tapping points. An example of a 9-stage shift-register p.r.b.s. generator is given in Fig.6.10. Note that for single intermediate tapping-point sequence generators, it turns out that the use of the intermediate feed-back point (n - m) instead of m will generate a similar sequence of length 2n - 1, but in the reverse order.

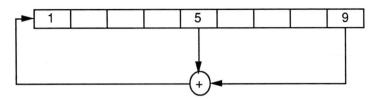

Fig.6.10 - 9-stage p.r.b.s. generator.

6.5.2 Self-Synchronizing Scramblers/Descramblers

One way of using the pseudo-random sequence concept to randomize (scramble) the transmitted data sequence is to simply add, modulo-2, the data and the sequence generated by an independent shift-register generator. However, to descramble, it will be necessary to have an identical shift-register generator at the receiver, operating in the same phase, in order to effect the descrambling. The problem is how to obtain and then to maintain the same sequence phase at both the transmitter and the receiver. To avoid this problem, the self-synchronizing scrambler-descrambler combination proposed by Savage [7] is used.

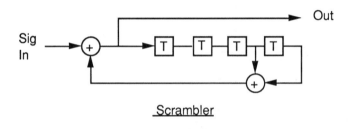

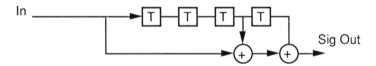

Fig.6.11 - Self-synchronizing scrambler-descrambler.

The scrambler and the descrambler each consist of a shift-register similar to that used for the p.r.b.s. generator, but the signals to be operated on are introduced directly into the feed-back path as shown in Fig.6.11. Clearly, with an all-zero input, the scrambler in effect becomes a conventional p.r.b.s. generator. Savage has shown that, for a periodic signal input, the line sequence period will be the lowest common multiple (LCM) of the corresponding p.r.b.s. and the input signal periods.

There is a small, but finite, chance of 'lock-up' if the all-zero sequence enters the register and is then maintained by an all-zero input. The larger n, the smaller this probability becomes and, for typical scrambler shift-register lengths of 22, it can safely be neglected. It will be seen that the sequence input into both the scrambler and descrambler shift-registers are identical (assuming no errors in transmission) and thus the two will be synchronized once n bits have been transmitted through the channel. This usually occurs during set-up, so no data is lost in practice during this synchronization interval.

If an error occurs in transmission, it will affect the descrambled data as it passes through each tapping point of the shift-register. For this reason it is important to minimize, as far as possible, the number of taps used. Using the polynomials with minimum taps, each error in transmission will give rise to up to three errors in the descrambler output. This error propagation is one of the penalties we have to pay for the convenience of using the self-synchronizing data scrambler-descrambler.

6.5.3 Encryption

The scrambler/descrambler combination described above can be used for simple encryption. However, the range of coding schemes available is such that it is not a difficult task to break the cipher. It can, however, be useful for the avoidance of casual eavesdropping.

For more secure encryption, a technique is used known as the Data Encryption Standard (DES) [8]. In the DES algorithm, the data is firstly broken up into blocks of 64 bits each. A key consisting of 56 bits is then used to encrypt each block individually. The same key is then used by the receivers to perform the inverse operation to decode the received data block. The use of a 56 bit key gives the choice of a possible 10^7 different keys, which is adequate enough for most commercial purposes.

The key is used to specify a sequence of transposition and substitution operations. In the transposition operations, the bits in the block are transposed into a different order. In the substitution operations, the complete set of bits are replaced by a different set of bits, determined mathematically from the original set of bits based on rules derived the key code bit pattern. The DES encoding procedure is shown in Fig.6.12.

The 56 bit key is used to derive 16 different subkeys, each of 48 bits. The algorithm consists of 19 steps. Firstly, there is a simple transposition operation, which is followed by 16 substitution operations based on the 16 subkeys derived from the 56 bit key. The most significant and least significant 32 bits of the last substitution are then transposed and the same transposition as was performed initially is then repeated. The received block is then decoded using the same steps in the receiver, but in the reverse order. This mode of working is often referred to as Electronic Code Book (ECB) because each message block has a unique matching code block in a way similar to entries in a code book.

The ECB mode of operation gives reasonable data protection for many applications. However, it does suffer from some deficiencies. Firstly, there is the possibility of inserting additional correctly enciphered blocks in the message, which would be undetectable by the receiver. Also repetitive blocks of message data generate a similarly repetitive stream of encoded data blocks, which can be very helpful to anyone trying to break the code. These deficiencies can be overcome by the use of chaining. In this scheme, each 64 bit message block is exclusive-ORed with the encoded output of the previous block before it is enciphered. This is illustrated in Fig.6.13.

The output of each block is thus a function of both the block itself and the encoded output of the previous block. Any alterations to the transmitted sequence are therefore apparent at the receiver and identical blocks of message data lead to different encoded output blocks. This mode of operation is therefore particularly attractive for secure data communication purposes.

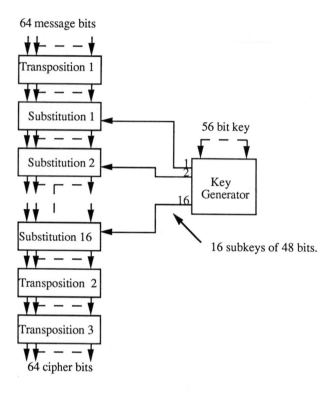

Fig.6.12 - The Data Encryption Standard (DES) Algorithm.

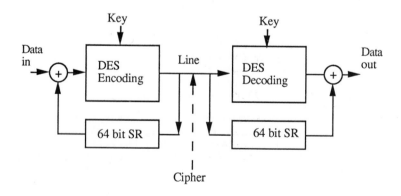

Fig.6.13 - Chaining Algorithm.

6.5.4 Public Key Systems

The methods of encryption described so far depend on the same key being used for both encoding and decoding. This means that both parties in a transmission must know the key and thus a key directory needs to be maintained. Thus security of keys becomes a problem. This can be partly overcome by regular changing of keys, but this also means regular notification of changes to all users. To overcome this problem, the Public Key System has been evolved. In the public key system, each message is encoded using two keys, known as the public key and the private key. The two keys are derived so that messages encoded using a receiver's public key can only be decoded using the receiver's private key. The keys are generated in such a way that ensures that the private key cannot be derived from knowledge of the public key. Thus the private key is known only to the recipient of the encoded message, whereas the public key can be published to all users. However, messages encoded using the public key cannot be decoded except by the possessor of the matching private key. The operation of the public key system is illustrated in Fig.6.14(a).

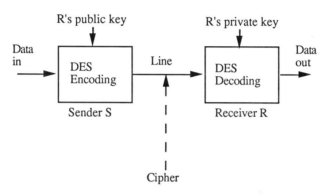

(a) Basic operation

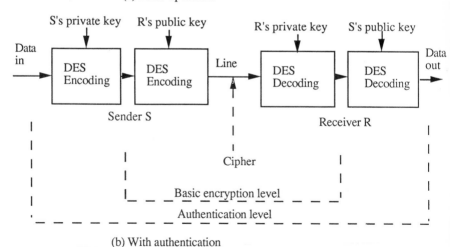

(b) With authentication

Fig.6.14 - Public Key System Operation.

The public key system can be used for message authentication as shown in Fig.6.14(b). The operation of the authentication procedure depends on the duality property of the coding scheme, which means that not only is a receiver able to decode all messages it receives using its own private key, but it can also decode a message encoded with the sender's private key using the sender's public key. The inner level of encoding is as described previously. However, the sender first uses its own private key to encode the original message. Thus, if the receiver is able to decode the message using the appropriate sender's public key, he is reasonably assured that the message was in fact originated by that sender.

A detailed discussion of Public Key Systems is to be found in Tanenbaum [9].

6.6   References

1.   Huffman, D., "A method for the construction of minimum redundancy codes", Proc. IRE. 40, 1952, pp 1098-1101.

2.   Wade, J.G., "Signal coding and processing", Ellis Horwood, 1987.

3.   Hagelbarger, D.W., "Recurrent codes: easily mechanized, burst-correcting binary codes", BSTJ., 38, 1959, pp 969-984.

4.   Duc, N.Q., and Smith, B.M., "Line coding for digital data transmission", Aust. Telecom. Rev., 11, 1977, pp 14-27.

5.   Crozier, A, "Introduction to pseudo-ternary transmission codes", IBM Journal Res.Dev., 14, 1970.

6.   Kretzmer, E.R., "Generalization of a technique for binary data communication", IEEE Trans. Comm., 14, 1976, pp 67-68.

7.   Savage, J.E., "Some simple self-synchronizing digital data scramblers", BSTJ., 46, 1967, pp 449-487.

8.   National Bureau of Standards (USA), "Data encryption standard", FIPS publication 46, 1983.

9.   Tanenbaum, A.S., "Computer Networks", Prentice Hall, 1981.

Further general reading:

10.   Brewster, R.L., "Communication systems and Computer Networks", Ellis Horwood, 1989.

11.   Bylanski, P, and Ingram, D.G.W. "Digital Transmission Systems", Peter Peregrinus, 1976.

Chapter 7

Data Transmission Standards and Interfaces

A. Clark

7.1 WHAT ARE STANDARDS?

A standard aims to achieve some form of compatibility or interoperability by specifying the technical characteristics necessary to fulfil that goal. An example of this is the standardized metric thread, which is widely used on a range of screws and bolts. Those of us who remember the days of Whitworth, BSF, BSP, BA, UNF, UNC, and more specialized threads, are able to recognize the benefits of standardization in terms of reduced "frustration factor". Another simple example of a standard is that set by the publishers of this book. A specification was provided to each contributor, describing the format of heading, paragraphs, and diagrams, the aim being to produce a consistent form throughout the book.

More formally, a Standard is a technical specification drawn up with the cooperation and approval of all interests affected by it, aimed at the promotion of community benefits, and approved by a body recognized on the national, regional or international level.

A *De Jure* standard (literally *by right*) is set by a formally constituted standards organization. It may be an international standard set by ISO (International Standards Organization), or in the telecommunications world by the ITU (International Telecommunications Union). It may be a national or regional standard, a standard set by a trade association, or even an internal company standard.

A *De Facto* standard (literally *in fact*) is a standard which has been adopted informally. It is often a proprietary scheme which has been widely used because there is no equivalent *de jure* standard. An example of this is the well known AT command set for the control of dial-up asynchronous modems.

The process of developing a standard is time consuming (often taking five years or more) and expensive. One may reasonably question whether the benefits offered outweigh the costs, however in the field of telecommunications there are a number of significant advantages:-

(i) Data transmission and interface standards permit systems (computers and terminals) to be interconnected, and in the field of information technology this is vital. An illustration of the importance of this may be seen in the facsimile machine, if no standards for facsimile transmission existed the medium would be very little used as only machines from the same manufacturer could communicate, however the existence of standards have made it one of the most important data communications media. There are many other examples, including the V.24/RS232 interface, the V.21/V.23 modem, and the HDLC protocols.

(ii) Standards remove dependence on particular suppliers. In fact standards are sometimes deliberately *not* used, in order to *lock customers in* to a particular system. Users of data communications equipment would generally prefer to be free to buy from multiple vendors, both on economic grounds (as competition brings prices down), and to reduce dependence on the fortunes of the equipment supplier.

(iii) Standards provide some guarantee of quality, as they are reviewed and evaluated by many technical experts before being approved. Formal specification and verification techniques are being applied to many of ISO and CCITT communications protocols, which would be beyond the resources of most individual companies. Test facilities are being established throughout the world in order that data communications products may be tested for conformity to standards.

(iv) International standards can remove barriers to trade caused by differences in national practices. This is particularly significant in Europe, as discussed later in this chapter.

(v) Safety, and the protection of the environment may be ensured. Currently new standards for telecommunications equipment safety and electromagnetic interference are being put in place.

Within this chapter the organization of the telecommunications standards world, and in particular the evolution of the standards organization within Europe, is discussed. This is followed by an outline of the process by which standards are developed, and a discussion of some of the more important data transmission and interface standards.

7.2   THE ORGANIZATION OF THE TELECOMMUNICATIONS STANDARDS WORLD

7.2.1 The who's who of the standards world

The telecommunications standards world is fairly well populated with committees, technical sub-committees, working groups, rapporteurs and editors. There is a considerable degree of cooperation between the different standards organizations, resulting in steps to rationalize the development of new standards.

This section introduces the key standards organizations involved in data communications, ISO, IEC, ITU, CCITT, and some of the regional and national organizations.

7.2.2   International Standards Organization

The International Standards Organization (ISO) was founded in 1947. It has headquarters in Geneva, and secretariats in a number of countries. ISO has more than 2000 technical committees for the preparation of international standards.

7.2.3   International Electrotechnical Commission

The International Electrotechnical Commission (IEC) was founded in 1906. It is the electrotechnical counterpart of ISO, concentrating on electronic equipment, electrical engineering, and industrial process control.

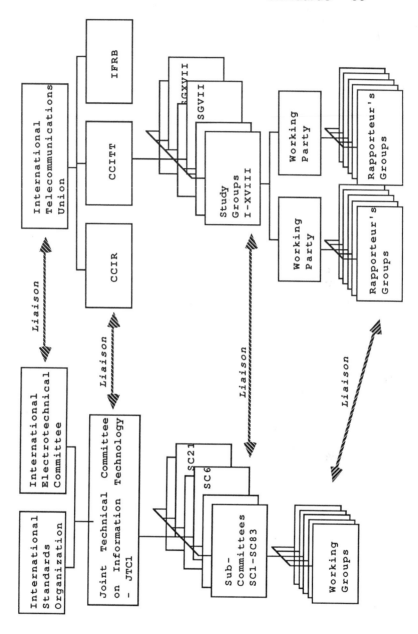

Fig.7.1. The Relationship between ISO and CCITT Standards Committees in the field of Data Communications

7.2.4   ISO/IEC Joint Technical Committee on Information Technology

In 1987 the information technology standardization activities of ISO and IEC were merged to form the ISO/IEC JTC1 joint technical committee. JTC1 has a number of sub-committees, each covering an aspect of information technology. Of the 17 or so sub-committees of ISO/IEC JTC1 those of most relevance to data communications are:-

SC-6   Telecommunications and Information Exchange
between Systems.

SC-21   Information Retrieval, Transfer, and Management
for Open Systems Interconnection (OSI).

Each sub-committee has working groups responsible for the development of standards.

Sub-committee SC-6 has four working groups, WG1 is responsible for Data Link Layer standards, WG2 for Network Layer standards, WG3 for Physical Layer and WG4 for Transport Layer standards.
Sub-committee SC-21 has five working groups, WG1 is responsible for OSI Architecture, WG3 for Database, WG4 for OSI Management, WG5 for Specific Application Layer Services, and WG6 for OSI Session, Presentation and Common Application Services.

7.2.5   International Telecommunications Union

The International Telegraph Union (ITU) was founded in 1865, and was renamed the International Telecommunications Union in 1932. Currently 162 countries are members of the ITU, and send delegates to a Plenipotentiary Conference held every five years to revise the ITU Convention and elect key officers.
The functions of the ITU are:-

(i) to maintain and extend international cooperation for the improvement and rational use of telecommunications of all kinds.

(ii) to promote the development of technical facilities and their most efficient operation with a view to improving the efficiency of telecommunications services, increasing their usefulness and making them as far as possible generally available to the public.

(iii) to harmonize the actions of nations in the attainment of these common ends.

The ITU founded the International Telephone Consultative Committee (CCIF) in 1924, followed shortly by the International Telegraph Consultative Committee (CCIT). The CCIF and CCIT were merged in 1956 to form the CCITT - the Comité Consultatif International Télégraphique et Téléphonique.
The other elements of the ITU are the International Radio Consultative Committee (CCIR), founded in 1927, and the International Frequency Registration Board (IFRB), founded in 1947.
The two CCI's are separate bodies dealing with technical radio and technical telegraph and telephone problems. All member countries of the ITU can participate in their work, also certain private companies operating telecommunications services or manufacturing telecommunications equipment. Each CCI holds a Plenary Assembly every few years. The Plenary Assembly draws up a list of technical telecommunications subjects or "Questions", the study of which would lead to improvement in international radiocommunication or international telegraphy and

telephony. These Questions are then entrusted to a number of Study Groups, composed of experts from different countries.

The CCITT Study Groups which deal with issues of immediate interest to the data communications world, are principally SGVII, SGVIII, SGXVII and SGXVIII.

SGVII   Data Communication Networks *(X Series Recommendations)* including both packet and circuit switched networks, routing, OSI, OSI management, and network performance.

SGVIII   Terminal Equipment for Telematics Services *(T Series Recommendations)* including facsimile, videotex and document architectures.

SGXVII   Data Transmission over the Telephone Network *(V Series Recommendations),* including modems and ISDN terminal adaptors.

SGXVIII Digital Networks including ISDN *(G and I Series Recommendations)* including the ISDN architecture, reference models, protocols, bearer services, and access interfaces, ATM, network performance.

7.2.6   European Standards Organizations

The subject of European standards development is covered in more detail in a later section, however the key organizations are introduced below:-

CEN   the Comité Européen de Normalisation, which is the principal standards body within Europe, equivalent in scope to ISO. Founded in 1961 CEN comprises the national standards bodies of the 16 EEC and EFTA countries.

CENELEC the Comité Européen de Normalisation Electrotechnique (founded 1973), which is the principal standards body within Europe in the field of electronics and information technology.

CEPT   the Conférence Européenne des Administrations des Postes et Télécommunications, which is the forum within which European agreements and standards relating to the public telecommunications network are established.

ETSI   the European Telecommunications Standards Institute, which was established in 1988 to develop standards in the field of telecommunications.

ECMA   the European Computer Manufacturers Association, which develops standards in the field of information technology, data communications, and private voice/data networks.

EWOS   the European Workshop on Open Systems, was founded at the end of 1987 by eight European organizations, with the support of the EEC and EFTA. Its aim is to be the structure and focal point in Europe for the development of OSI profiles and corresponding test specifications.

7.2.7 Telecommunications Standards Organizations in the UK

Within the UK, the principal standards authorities are the Department of Trade and Industry, and the British Standards Institute.

The British Standards Institute is an independent organization, incorporated under Royal Charter. It is the recognized body in the UK for the preparation and promulgation of national standards in all fields. It is recognized as the UK representative to ISO, IEC, CEN, and CENELEC.

The BSI T/- Council for Automation and Information Technologies has an Information Systems Technology Standards Committee (BSI IST/-) which parallels the ISO/IEC JTC1 committee. The sub-committees of BSI IST/- correspond to those of JTC1.

The UK as a Telecommunications Administration is represented by the Department of Trade and Industry, whose role is primarily policy and coordination. DTI run committees such as the Telecommunications Attachments Policy Committee (TAPC). The DTI have the responsibility for representing the UK within major telecommunications organizations such as ITU, CCITT, CCIR, and CEPT. The views of UK industry are coordinated by *coordination committees*, with coordinators appointed by the DTI. There are, for example, coordination committees for CCITT SGXVII and SGXVIII which meet regularly during Study Periods to for UK views on current issues and discuss progress in CCITT meetings.

The UK manufacturers associations most closely associated with data communications are the Telecommunications Equipment Manufacturers Association (TEMA), the Business Equipment and Information Technology Association (BEITA) and the Electronic Engineering Association (EEA).

7.2.8 Telecommunications Standards in the USA

The principal standards organization in the USA is the American National Standards Institute (ANSI). Standards development is undertaken by *accredited standards committees* (ASC's), sponsored by associations such as ECSA and EIA.

Telecommunications standards are developed principally by three ANSI committees:-

(i) T1, which is sponsored by the Exchange Carriers Standards Association (ECSA). There are a number of technical sub-committees of T1, including T1S1 which studies ISDN, and T1M1 which studies maintenance.

(ii) X3, which is sponsored by the Computer and Business Equipment Manufacturers Association (CBEMA). X3 has a number of technical advisory groups which cover all aspects of information systems, committee X3S3 studies data communications (equating to ISO/IEC JTC1 SC6).

(iii) TR30, which is sponsored by the Electronic Industries Association (EIA), and studies data transmission systems and equipment.

In addition, the Institute of Electrical and Electronic Engineers (IEEE) is actively involved in the development of standards, particularly in the area of local area networks, interfaces, busses, and software development.

7.3   THE EUROPEAN DIMENSION

The European Commission have taken an active interest in the development of information technology and telecommunications standards. The Commission set out programmes of work on common technical specifications (Normes Européennes de Télécommunications - NETs) and established an advisory committee, the Senior Officials Group for Telecommunications (SOGT), to assist them in managing the programmes of work.

The objectives are:-

(i) To develop an open market in Europe for terminal equipment.

(ii) To encourage the prompt implementation of OSI.

A subsequent EEC *Decision* which has far reaching consequences within Europe in the field of IT products and means for access to data services provided over public networks was made in 1987. The Decision stated that there would be regular reviews of standardization priorities, that European standards institutions and specialized technical bodies would be requested to collaborate in preparing *European Standards* (EN's), that there would be coordination of verification and conformance testing facilities, and that Member States would have to ensure that reference is made to European and International Standards in public procurement orders. A new advisory committee was established, the Senior Officials Group on standardization in the field of Information Technology (SOGITS).

In order to achieve its objectives the Commission initiated three projects to develop Functional Standards, Conformance Testing/Certification, and NETs (European Telecommunications Standards).

(i) Functional Standards, recommend how to provide a particular function using certain international standards.   Functional standards will promote OSI communications, but do not define the procedures for attachment to the different European networks.

(ii) Conformance Testing/Certification, fulfils the need to test IT products for conformity to standards, and provide harmonized European certificates of conformity

(iii) European Telecommunications Standards, or NETs, specify the interface between terminal equipment and the public network. Compliance to NETs will be obligatory within the EEC and most CEPT member countries, and once an item of equipment has been tested for conformance to a NET in one country, the results of the test will be accepted in the other supporting countries.

NETs fall into two basic classes, *Access NETS*, which are intended to ensure that no disturbance occurs to the network, and that calls can be routed successfully, *Terminal NETs*, which ensure end to end compatibility of a defined communications service.

Each year a list of priorities for the development of new European Telecommunications Standards (NETs) will be drawn up by the Commission in consultation with the SOGT advisory committee and the CEPT Harmonization Coordination Committee (CCH).

The CEPT Technical Recommendations Application Committee (TRAC) determines which aspect of the standards will be mandatory. The standard is developed as a *recommendation* by the sub-technical-committees of the European Telecommunications Standards Institute (ETSI) and then approved by TRAC as a NET.

The work program for Functional Standards is developed by the joint CEN/CENELEC/CEPT information technology committees, ITSTC (Information Technology Steering Committee) and ITAEGS (Information Technology Ad Hoc Experts Group on Standardization).

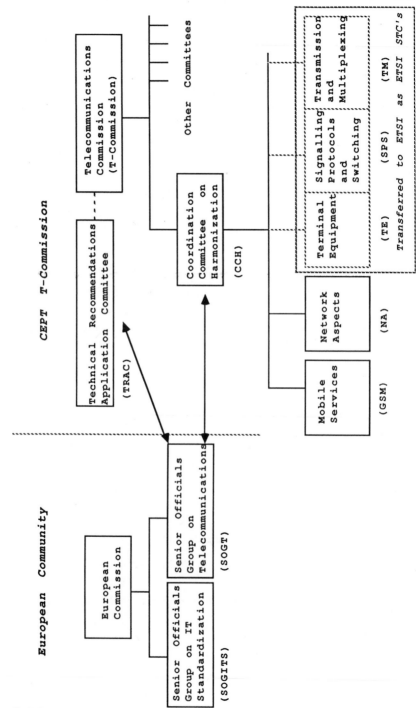

Fig.7.2.   Relationship between EEC and CEPT

7.4   DEVELOPING A STANDARD

7.4.1 Originating the idea

The need for a standard may be identified in several different ways. It may arise from a planning exercise by one of the standards organizations, may be the result of a request by a industrial organization for study in a particular area, or may be the recognition of a *de facto* standard. When a work area has been identified, the process of developing the standard may commence.

7.4.2 Development of a CCITT Recommendation

CCITT operates in four year cycles or Study Periods, for example 1984-1988 and 1988-1992. At the end a Study Period the Recommendations drawn up during the 4 year period are approved by the Plenary Assembly, and are then published in a set of *coloured* books. A different colour is adopted in each Study Period, hence the colour of the publications is often used to refer to the series; the Red Books were published following the 1980-84 Study Period, and the Blue Books following the 1984-88 Study Period.

The Questions (defined above) are established by the Plenary Assembly, in practice as a result of proposals by the Study Groups. Each Question is studied by a Rapporteur's Group (experts group) which meets sufficiently often to progress work (say 2-4 times/year). The Study Groups draw up Recommendations which are submitted to the next Plenary Assembly.

An *accelerated procedure* exists for Recommendations which are needed urgently, which allows approval to obtained in about seven months. CCITT are beginning to encourage the use of the accelerated procedure as a way of reducing the workload at the end of a Study Period.

7.4.3 Development of an ISO/IEC JTC1 Standard

There are five successive stages of technical work within JTC1:-

(i)   A proposal for a *New Work Item* is circulated to members of JTC1, following which work may commence.

(ii)   A *working draft* is developed within a Working Group.

(iii) When a document is at a sufficiently advanced stage, it may be submitted as a *Draft Proposal* (DP) to members of JTC1 or one of its sub-committees for comment and vote.

(iv) When there is substantial support for the DP, possibly after revision to accommodate comments of members, it may go forward as a *Draft International Standard* (DIS) for circulation to national bodies for approval.

(v)   When a DIS has received the support of the majority of JTC1 members, and at least 75% of the voting national bodies, it may go forward for publication as an *International Standard* (IS).

In addition a *fast-track* procedure exists to allow existing standards from other organization to be submitted directly for vote as DIS.

7.4.4   Commercial versus technical considerations

Although a substantial part of the international standards community comprises officials from government and national standards organizations, many of the working groups are formed from experts from industry. This has substantial advantages to both the standards committee, in that expertise and resource is available to progress the work, and to the manufacturers themselves, as they are able to influence the direction of the development of a standard. In general, although there are often strong commercial interests in the development of a standard, these are manifested only in terms of delay rather than exploitation of the standard.

Another aspect of standards development that may result in conflict between commercial and technical interests relates to intellectual property. Both CCITT and ISO/IEC JTC1 request that companies holding patents which may cover some aspect of a standard make a statement relating to the availability of licenses. The usual statement is that the company is prepared to make licenses available on reasonable and non-discriminatory terms.

7.5   DATA COMMUNICATIONS STANDARDS

7.5.1 Data Communications Standards in Action

The main CCITT and ISO standards relating to data transmission and interfaces are listed below, however this section illustrates how standards are applied in practice.

Any data communications product will have to conform to a number of different standards. For example, a V.32 modem is shown below, with some of the relevant standards marked.

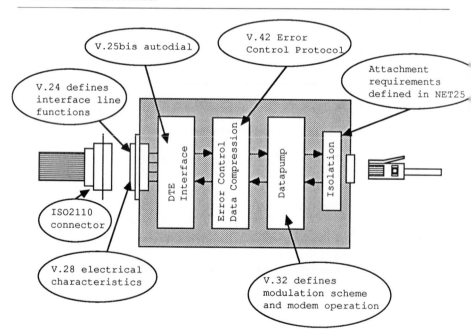

Fig.7.3   Standards in Action .. a V.32 Modem

Progressing from left to right, the modem must comply with:-

ISO2110   which specified the physical dimensions and pin assignment for the 25 way "D" type connector.

V.24   which lists the interface circuits and identifies their function.

V.28   which specifies the electrical characteristics of the interface circuits.

V.25bis   which specifies the protocol used by a terminal to communicate with the modem for the purpose of automatic dialing.

V.42   which specifies the error control protocol used between a pair of modems.

V.32   which defines the modulation scheme used by the modem, and the means for establishing a connection.

NET25   (when approved) which specifies the European requirements for attachment to the PSTN, including safety and interference requirements, and the requirements for conformance to V.32.

In addition, the modem will have to satisfy a large number of other standards relating to electrical safety, electromagnetic radiation, flammability, and component standards.

7.5.2 CCITT Recommendations relating to data communications

V Series Recommendations, developed by CCITT SGXVII

The V series Recommendations cover three main areas, modems (e.g.V.21, V.22, V.22bis, V.23, V.32...), interfaces (e.g. V.24, V.35, V.230) and V series ISDN terminal adaptors (V.110, V.120). The most widely known V series Recommendations are the V.24 interface and the V.22bis modem.

V.10   Electrical characteristics for unbalanced double- current interchange circuits for general use with integrated circuit equipment in the field of data communications.

V.11   Electrical characteristics for balanced double- current interchange circuits for general use with integrated circuit equipment in the field of data communications.

V.13   Simulated carrier control.

V.14   Transmission of start-stop mode characters over synchronous bearer channels.

V.21   300 bit/s duplex modem standardized for use in the general switched network.

V.22   1200 bit/s duplex modem standardized for use in the general switched network and on point-to-point 2-wire leased telephone type circuits.

V.22bis   2400 bit/s duplex modem using the Frequency Division technique standardized for use in the general switched network and on point-to-point 2-wire leased telephone type circuits.

V.23	600/1200-baud modem standardized for use in the general switched network.
V.24	List of definitions for interchange circuits between data terminal equipment and data circuit terminating equipment.
V.25bis	Automatic calling and/or answering equipment on the general switched telephone network (GSTN) using the 100 series interchange circuits.
V.26	2400 bit/s modem standardized for use on 4-wire leased telephone-type circuits.
V.26bis	2400/1200 bit/s modem standardized for use in the general switched telephone network
V.26ter	2400 bit/s modem using the echo cancellation technique standardized for use in the general switched network and on point-to-point 2-wire leased telephone type circuits.
V.27	4800 bit/s modem with manual equalizer standardized for use on leased telephone-type circuits.
V.27bis	4800/2400 bit/s modem with automatic equalizer standardized for use on leased telephone-type circuits.
V.27ter	4800/2400 bit/s modem with automatic equalizer standardized for use in the general switched network.
V.28	Electrical characteristics for unbalanced double current interchange circuits.
V.29	9600 bit/s modem standardized for use on point-to-point 4-wire leased telephone-type circuits.
V.32	9600 bit/s duplex modem standardized for use on the general switched telephone network and on leased telephone type circuits.
V.33	14400 bit/s modem standardized for use on point-to-point 4-wire leased telephone-type circuits.
V.35	Data transmission at 48 kilobits per second using 60-108 kHz group band circuits.
V.42	Error-Correcting Procedures for DCEs using Asynchronous to Synchronous Conversion.
V.54	Loop test devices for modems.
V.110	Support of data terminal equipments (DTEs) with V series type interfaces by an integrated services digital network (ISDN).
V.120	Support by an ISDN of Data Terminal Equipment with V series type interfaces with provision for statistical multiplexing.
V.230	General data communications interface.

X Series Recommendations, developed by CCITT SGVII

The X series Recommendations cover various aspects of data networks, including interfaces, network performance, routing and OSI. The most widely known X series Recommendations are X.21, which is a synchronous terminal interface, and X.25, which is an interface between a packet mode terminal and a packet network.

X.20
: Interface between data terminal equipment (DTE) and data circuit terminating equipment (DCE) for start-stop transmission services on public data networks.

X.20bis
: Use on public data networks of data terminal equipment (DTE) which is designed for interfacing to asynchronous duplex V series modems.

X.21
: Interface between data terminal equipment (DTE) and data circuit terminating equipment (DCE) for synchronous operation on public data networks.

X.21bis
: Use on public data networks of data terminal equipment (DTE) which is designed for interfacing to synchronous V series modems.

X.22
: Multiplex DTE/DCE interface for user classes 3-6.

X.24
: List of definitions for interchange circuits between data terminal equipment (DTE) and data circuit terminating equipment (DCE) on public data networks.

X.25
: Interface between data terminal equipment (DTE) and data circuit terminating equipment (DCE) for terminals operating in the packet mode and connected to public data networks by dedicated circuits.

X.26
: Electrical characteristics for unbalanced double- current interchange circuits for general use with integrated circuit equipment in the field of data communications.

X.27
: Electrical characteristics for balanced double- current interchange circuits for general use with integrated circuit equipment in the field of data communications.

X.28
: DTE/DCE interface for a start-stop mode data terminal equipment accessing the packet assembly/disassembly facility (PAD) in a public data network situated in the same country.

X.29
: Procedures for the exchange of control information and user data between a packet assembly/disassembly facility (PAD) and a packet mode DTE or another PAD.

X.30
: Support of X.21 and X.21bis based data terminal equipment (DTEs) by an integrated services digital network (ISDN).

X.31
: Support of packet mode terminal equipment by an ISDN.

X.32
: Interface between a data terminal equipment (DTE) and data circuit terminating equipment (DCE) for terminals operating in the packet mode and accessing a packet switched public data network through a public switched telephone network or a circuit switched public data network.

7.5.3   ISO Data Communications Standards

Of the ISO data communications standards many are in use, however the most widely recognized is probably HDLC, the High Level Data Link Control procedure (ISO 3309, 7809,...). This provides a set of elements which may be used to build data link level (layer 2) protocols such as X.25 layer 2, or V.42.

ISO2110	25 pin DTE/DCE interface connector and pin assignments.
ISO2593	34 pin DTE/DCE interface connector and pin assignments.
ISO3309	High Level Data Link Control Procedures - Frame Structure.
ISO4335	High Level Data Link Control Procedures - Elements of Procedure.
ISO4902	37 pin DTE/DCE interface connector and pin assignments.
ISO4903	15 pin DTE/DCE interface connector and pin assignments.
ISO7809	High Level Data Link Control Procedures - Consolidation of Classes of Procedure.
ISO7776	High Level Data Link Control Procedures - Description of the X.25 LAPB compatible DTE data link procedures.
ISO8208	X.25 Packet Layer Protocol for data terminal equipment.
ISO8348	Network Service Definition.
ISO8473	Protocol for providing the connectionless mode Network Service.
ISO8802-2	Local Area Networks - Part 2 Logical Link Control.
ISO8802-3	Local Area Networks - Part 3 CSMA/CD Access Method and Physical Layer Specifications.
ISO8802-4	Local Area Networks - Part 4 Token Passing Bus Access Method and Physical Layer Specifications.
ISO8802-5	Local Area Networks - Part 5 Token Ring Access Method and Physical Layer Specifications.
ISO8802-7	Local Area Networks - Part 7 Slotted Ring Access Method and Physical Layer Specifications.
ISO8877	Interface Connector and Contact Assignments for ISDN Basic Access Interface Located at Reference Points S and T.
ISO8878	Use of X.25 to provide the OSI Connection Oriented Network Service.
ISO8880	Specification of Protocols to Provide and Support the OSI Network Service.
ISO8881	Use of the X.25 Packet Layer Protocol in ISO 8802 Local Area Networks.

ISO8885   High Level Data Link Control Procedures - General Purpose XID
           Frame Information Field and Content.

ISO8886   Data Link Service Definition for Open Systems Interconnection.

7.5.4   European Standards

At the time of preparation of this chapter the NETs shown below were not
complete.

NET1   X.21 Access, ... interface and access control protocol to be offered
           by terminal equipment at an interface to a public switched
           telecommunication network or a leased circuit provided by a public
           network operator.

NET2   X.25 Access, ... interface and access control protocol to be offered
           by terminal equipment at an interface to a public telecommunications
           network.

NET3   ISDN Basic Access, ... interface and access control protocol to be
           offered by terminal equipment at an interface to a public
           telecommunications network at an ISDN basic access point.

NET4   PSTN Basic Access, ... interface and method of signalling to be
           offered by voice or non-voice terminal equipment at an analogue
           interface to a public switched telephone network. It is likely that for
           some time to come this NET will specify a number of national
           variants, rather than a common standard.

NET5   ISDN Primary Rate Access, ... interface and access control protocol
           to be offered by terminal equipment at an interface to a public
           network at an ISDN primary rate (2048 kbit/s) access point.

NET6   Switched Access to PSPDN (X.32), ... interface and access protocol
           to be used by packet mode terminal equipment when accessing a
           PSPDN via a PSTN, CSPDN or ISDN circuit.

NET7   ISDN Terminal Adaptor, ... technical characteristics of terminal
           equipment which will be connected to ISDN basic access points to
           provide terminal adaption to a DTE/DCE interface.

NET10   European 900 MHz Digital Cellular Mobile Telecommunications
           Network Access, ... technical characteristics (radio frequency,
           modulation, method of access and signalling) to be offered by voice or
           non-voice terminal equipment at the radio interface to a European
           900MHz digital cellular mobile telecommunications network.

NET20   General Requirements for Voice Band Modems, ... specifies
           technical characteristics (safety, protection of network, no interference
           with other users) of the PSTN interface of a terminal which transmits
           or receives data signals in the voice band.

NET21   Specific Requirements for Modem V.21, ... requirements and
           compliance tests necessary to ensure end to end interoperability and
           verify conformance with the relevant parts of CCITT
           Recommendation V.21.

NET22   Specific Requirements for Modem V.22, ... (as for NET21).

NET23   Specific Requirements for Modem V.22bis, ... (as for NET21).

NET24   Specific Requirements for Modem V.23, ... (as for NET21).

NET25   Requirements for Modem V.32.

NET30-32   Facsimile and Teletext.

7.5.5   Other Interface Standards

The IEEE802 series of LAN standards have proved formative in the development of local area networks. Most of the established IEEE802 series standards have been adopted by ISO, as the ISO 8802 series standards.

The Electronic Industries Association (EIA) developed a number of interfaces, including RS232C, RS422, RS423, and more recently RS232D and RS530.

7.6   SUMMARY

Standards are essential to the data communications industry. It is becoming more apparent that an understanding of the process by which standards are developed is important to manufacturers, as they must ensure that they:-

- understand which standards are important to the market that they wish to address.

- ensure that standards being developed are commercially viable and technically feasible.

- are aware of standards being developed which may affect products being designed.

An understanding of the standards development process is equally important to the user or customer as they:-

- need to be aware of standards being developed which may affect their system and network purchases.

- can make ensure that standards being developed meet their needs.

- can initiate standardization activity in areas of concern.

- can have confidence in the migration of their systems towards OSI.

- can insist on conformance to established standards.

Chapter 8

ISDN

J. Hovell

8.1 INTRODUCTION

The initial ideas on ISDN were formulated about 12 years ago and reached some maturity with the publication of the CCITT "Red Book" in 1984. This has lead to ISDN becoming a world-wide reality today.

One of the reasons for this rapid emergence of ISDNs is the substantial growth and convergence of the Telecommunications and Information Technology industries. However the main driving force is technological; ISDN is a natural progression from the digitization of telephone networks.

Starting in the sixties we first saw the introduction of PCM into the inter-exchange transmission links. Following this came digital switching which resulted in Integrated Digital Networks (IDNs). Most developed countries throughout the world now have an IDN that supports telephony at 64 kbit/s.

It was realized that IDNs could be adapted to carry not only the telephone service but also many other services currently provided by other networks or that may be provided in the future, including data services. The development of IDNs into Integrated Service Digital Networks (ISDNs) is now occurring.

8.2. ISDN PRINCIPLES

The CCITT definition of an ISDN is:

"An ISDN is a network, in general evolving from a telephony IDN, that provides end-to-end digital connectivity to support a wide range of services, including voice and non-voice services, to which users have access by a limited set of standard multi-purpose user-network interfaces"

From this description it can be seen that an ISDN may be implemented in two ways, either as a new homogeneous network such as proposed in Australia or as the provision of a common access for all services but with the services supported on separate, service dedicated, networks. For example these may be the Public Switched Telephone Network (PSTN) for telephony, a packet network and a viewdata network. The second approach is the most common with an evolution towards integrating networks envisaged, such as the packet network with the telephony IDN.

The end-to-end digital connectivity is provided by extending IDNs to the customer by digital transmission between the main network and the customer. This final digital link is known as integrated digital access.

CCITT have specified ISDN access in terms of channels. The main types of channel are:

B Channels: 64 kbit/s channel for carrying user information such as voice encoded at 64 kbit/s or data information.

D Channel: either 16 or 64 kbit/s, primarily intended to carry signalling information for circuit switching. In addition to signalling it may carry packet switched data.

The two accesses recommended by CCITT being:

Basic rate access with a capability of 2B + D (16 kbit/s)

Primary rate access with a capability of 30 B (in 2 Mbit/s networks), or 23 B (in 1.5 Mbit/s networks) + D (64 kbit/s)

8.2.1   Basic Rate Access

Basic rate access provides two B channels and a 16 kbit/s D channel. Each B channel may have a different directory number depending on a service mark set at subscription time. Both B channels may carry voice or data up to 64 kbit/s.
This access uses the existing copper pair for transmission to the local switching centre.

8.2.2   Primary Rate Access

Primary rate access provides a 64 kbit/s D channel and up to thirty 64 kbit/s B channels carried on a 2 Mbit/s digital path (24 connections on 1.5 Mbit/s PCM systems in the US). Initially the principal expected use for primary rate access is for the connection of digital PABXs to the ISDN, such PBXs are known as Integrated Service PBXs or ISPBXs.
The 2 Mbit/s data stream is presented to the customer in accordance with CCITT recommendations G703 and G734. In these recommendations the bit stream comprises of 32 time slots with signalling (D channel) in timeslot 16 and alarms and framing information in timeslot 0.

8.2.3   Layered Model

One of the fundamental principles of the ISDN is the separation of signalling from the users data. In CCITT terms the signalling is in the Control or C-plane and the user data is in the User or U-plane. The signalling protocols in the C-plane are organized in three layers in accordance with ISO's reference model for Open Systems Interconnection (OSI):

Layer 1, the physical layer, is concerned with the physical circuit over which the signals are transmitted. Layer 1 is different for basic rate access and primary rate access interfaces. Basic rate access is defined in CCITT recommendation I430 and primary rate access in recommendation I431.

Layer 2, the link layer, is responsible for transferring signalling messages between the terminal and the network. Its main role is to detect and correct transmission errors that may have been introduced.

Layer 3, the network layer, is concerned with procedures for setting up and clearing down calls and controlling supplementary services.

Layers 2 and 3 are the same for both basic and primary rate accesses. Layer

2 is defined in CCITT recommendation I441 and layer 3 in recommendation I451.

8.2.4   ISDN Call Establishment

With reference to Fig.8.1. a simple call set up would be as follows. The customer requests a new call - the layer 3 process in the terminal forms a call request message (SETUP) and passes it to layer 2 for transmission to the layer 3 serving the local switch.

The layer 3 call control process in the switch makes a routing decision based on the called user address in the call request (SETUP) message, reserves a path through the switch, and sends a message to the next switch en route using the interexchange CCITT Signalling System No 7.

The call set up progresses through the network. At the destination end the call request (SETUP) is delivered to the called terminal and an indication (ALERT) returned to the caller that the called terminal is being alerted. If the call is accepted a call accepted (CONNECT) message is returned to the calling terminal. As this message passes through the network the reserved path is connected through and the connection is established. The conversation or data transfer then proceeds. Following a call set up either user may initiate cleardown at any time.

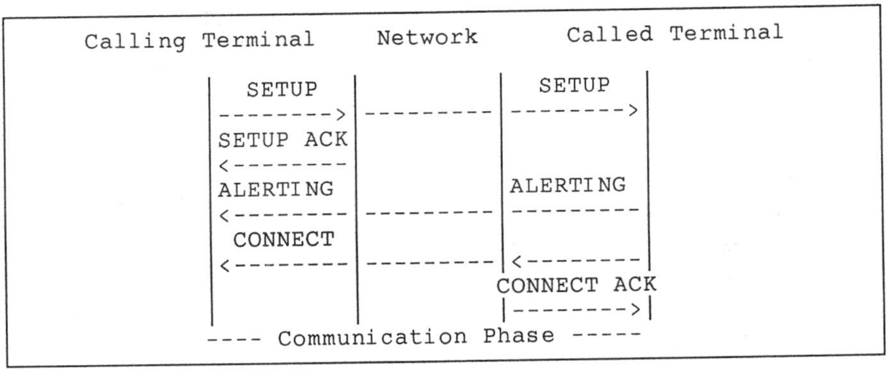

```
Calling Terminal    Network      Called Terminal

     |  SETUP   |           |  SETUP   |
     | -------->| --------- | -------->|
     | SETUP ACK|           |          |
     | <--------|           |          |
     | ALERTING |           | ALERTING |
     | <--------| --------- | -------- |
     | CONNECT  |           |          |
     | <--------| --------- | <--------|
     |          |           | CONNECT ACK
     |          |           | -------->|
     | ---- Communication Phase -----
```

Fig.8.1 - Signalling in the ISDN

8.3.   BASIC RATE ACCESS

8.3.1   Introduction

This chapter describes the I-series basic rate access as detailed in the I420 series of recommendations. The basic rate access is described as it contains more novel and interesting features than the primary rate access. The principles of the signalling apply equally to both access types and are described in section 4.

The CCITT reference configuration for the basic rate access user-network interface is shown in Fig.8.2. This illustrates the idea of functional groupings and reference points. The functional groupings are defined as:

NT1 (Network Termination 1) on its network side an NT1 terminates the two wire line from the local network and on the user side supports the S interface.

NT2 (Network Termination 2) provides functions to distribute the access to the customers network; PABXs and LANs are examples of NT2s.

TE1 (Terminal Equipment 1) is a terminal that has an I-series user-network interface.

TE2 (Terminal Equipment 2) is a terminal which does not have an I-series user-network interface but has an interface belonging to one of the data or analogue networks e.g. a CCITT X or V series interface.

TA (Terminal Adapter) performs the functions necessary to adapt the non-ISDN interface of a TE2 to the ISDN interface of a NT2.

Note that R, S and T are reference points and not physical interfaces since two or more functional groupings may be combined in a single piece of equipment. However if the TE1 and the NT2 are physically separate then the definition of the physical interface at the S reference point is the CCITT ISDN User/Network interface. The NT2 may be omitted, in which case the reference points S and T are coincident. Although S and T are strictly speaking "reference points at which a physical interfaces may occur" this often is abbreviated to the S interface.

In most countries a Network Termination owned by the service provider and located on the customers premises provides the customer with an I-series user-network interface. This is not the case in the USA where the regulatory position is that the user-network interface is the 2-wire line, the customer providing the NT1 functions

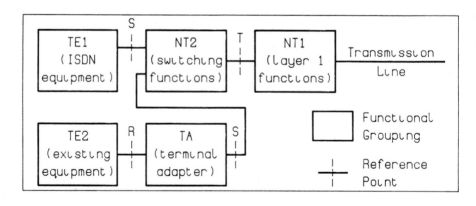

Fig.8.2 - User-network interface reference configuration

8.3.2   Customer Installation

An ISDN basic rate access customer's installation is represented pictorially in Fig.8.3. The ISDN network terminates in the NT1. In the UK the socket in the NT1 is the end of the network operators network and the beginning of the liberalized area. Into this NT1 is connected a four wire bus (the S interface) which may be configured either as either a point-to point or a point-to-multipoint arrangement. In the point-to-point configuration one terminal may be connected at the end of up to about 1 km of cable. In the point-to-multipoint configuration up to eight terminals may be connected in parallel anywhere along the bus, but the bus length is now limited to about 200 metres. This bus carries, in addition to the two B channels and the D channel, other bits used for miscellaneous purposes including frame synchronization.

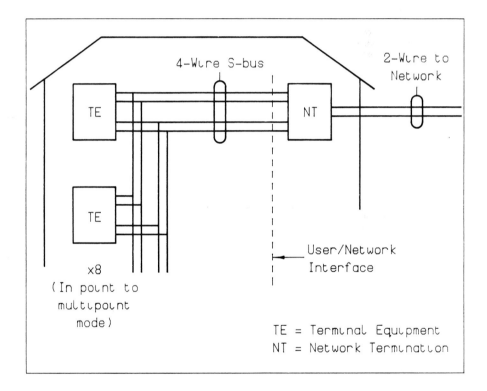

Fig.8.3 - Customers installation

8.3.3   Local Network Transmission

In the UK the existing local cable network connecting the local digital exchange to the customer is designed for a maximum attenuation of 15dB at 1600 Hz, the network being originally intended to carry analogue signals with a bandwidth of 4 kHz. Other countries have similar planning limits. Not only are these local cables used for only a short proportion of the time but, in general, the services they carry occupy only a small proportion of the bandwidth available. Fig.8.4 shows typical limits imposed by crosstalk on the capacity of these cables. This shows that, with practical systems, very nearly 100% of the existing network can support transmission at frequencies up to 100 kHz; hence ISDN basic rate access can be supported on the local network.

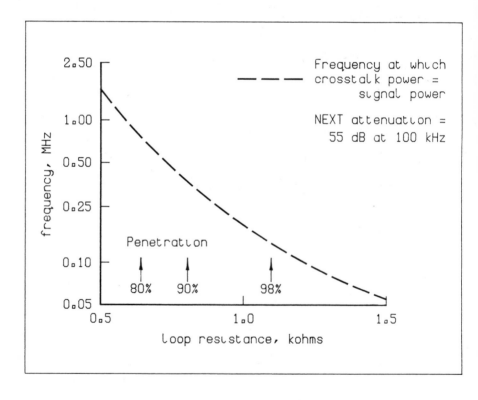

Fig.8.4 - Crosstalk limited bandwidth

The three principal methods of achieving full duplex transmission over a single pair cable are Burst Mode, Frequency Division and Echo Canceling. Echo canceling provides the lowest bandwidth and highest performance although it has the disadvantage of requiring relatively complex, large scale integrated circuits.

CCITT have not developed a recommendation for the transmission system to be used in the Local Network. This is largely because Network Providers did not wish the 2-wire line to be standardized as they believed it would open the way to the 2-wire line becoming a user-network interface. If this became the case it would not permit the local line transmission system to evolve without having an impact on the user-network interface.

In the US where the regulatory position has forced the ISDN user-network to be at the 2-wire line the line code 2B1Q has been selected as the national standard. This has resulted in a convergence of interest in this line code and several semiconductor device manufacturers have announced that they will introduce products compatible with this standard over the next few years.

8.3.4   Layer 1 of the User-Network Interface

8.3.4.1 Introduction. Layer 1 is responsible for transferring information from layer 2 of the terminal to the network. The transmission medium used to achieve this is the traditional building wiring from the terminal to the NT1 (i.e. twisted pair cable, within the customers premises) and the local network from the NT1 to the local exchange. Transmission over these media may well result in errors being introduced. It is Layer 2's function to apply any error detection and correction. Layer 1's responsibility is only transport the information at the physical level with acceptable quality.

8.3.4.2 Functions. In order for Layer 1 of the S interface to support Layer 2 it must have certain characteristics, the main characteristics are described below:

B Channels. Layer 1 must support, for each direction of transmission, two independent 64 kbit/s B channels. The B channels contain the user data which is switched by the network to provide an end to end transmission service. A B channel path is established by signalling messages in the D channel, each B channel being allocated to a particular terminal during call set-up.

D Channels. Layer 1 must support, for each direction of transmission, a 16 kbit/s channel for the signalling information. In some networks user packet data may also be supported on the D channel.

D Channel Access Procedure. This procedure ensures that in the case of two or more terminals on a point-to-multipoint configuration attempting to access the D channel simultaneously, one terminal will always successfully complete the transmission of information.

The procedure relies on the fact that the D channel is echoed back to the terminals from the NT in the D-echo channel. A terminal may only proceed to transmit on the D channel when it observes that the channel is not being used by a second terminal. Should a collision occur as a result of two (or more) terminals attempting to access the D channel simultaneously then the terminal that observes the corruption ceases transmission immediately.

Power Feeding. In the BT network a limited amount of power (called "restricted power") is provided from the network to the terminal in order, for example, to maintain a basic telephone service in the event of local power failure. In countries where the NT is mains powered, such as Germany, sufficient power for up to four terminals is provided. In the event of a failure of the mains power the interface reverts to restricted power.

Activation/Deactivation. Deactivation permits the TE and NT equipments to be placed in a low power mode when no calls are in progress; activation restores the equipment to its normal power mode. A low power mode is required for two purposes. Firstly to save power. This is significant from the network point of view as the NT1 is line powered. Deactivation is also provided to reduce electromagnetic radiation and hence crosstalk interference.

The interface may be activation from either the terminal and network side, but deactivated only from the network side because of the NT1's multi-terminal capability.

8.3.4.3 Binary organization of a layer 1 frame. The structures of the layer 1 frames across the S interface are different in each direction of transmission. Both structures are illustrated in Fig.8.5.

A frame contains 48 bits, is of 250 us duration, and is transmitted at a bit rate of 192 kbit/s.

In the direction terminal to network each frame consist of groups of bits, each group is DC balanced by its last bit (L bit). Each B and D channel group needs to be individually balanced as they may originate from different terminals. In addition to the groups formed by the B and D channels there are also groups formed by the framing and auxiliary framing bits, both bits being associated with a frame alignment procedure.

In the direction network to terminal, in addition to the B and D channel each frame also contains a D-echo channel (E-bits) used to return the D-bits to the terminals. The D-echo channel is used in the D channel contention procedure. The last bit of the frame (L-bit)is used to balance the complete frame. Other bits in the frame include the S-bit which is spare and the M-bit which may be used for multiframing, a facility not used in Europe.

The line code used is pseudo-ternary, a binary one is represented by no line signal and a binary zero by either a positive or a negative mark. The first binary zero following the frame balance bit is of the same polarity as that balance bit. Subsequent marks alternate in polarity. It is this violation of the alternate mark inversion of the framing bit and its balance bit that identifies the start of a frame.

8.3.4.4 Physical implementation. Semiconductor manufacturers are introducing devices to perform the functions described above. This is often in the form of two chips, one providing the transmission functions and the other digital logic. The first chip contains the transmitters and receivers with associated timing extraction, the second chip containing a frame formatter, channel multiplexing and demultiplexing and a micro processor interface for control of both chips. This second chip often also contains the basic functions of the layer 2 processing for the D channel.

To complete the circuitry a line transformer is used to provide a balanced line signal and dc isolation.

To protect the silicon from induced transients on the bus, protection diodes are required and ideally, some series impedance to dissipate the power.

8.4   SIGNALLING

8.4.1   Layer 2

The CCITT layer 2 recommendation I441 describes the procedures necessary for a Data Link access and is commonly referred to as the Link Access Procedure for the D channel or LAP D. The object of layer 2 is to provide an error free interchange of I441 frames between two end points connected by the physical medium. Layer 3 call control information is carried in the information elements of Layer 2 frames.

I441 frames consist of a sequence of octets as shown in fig.8.6.

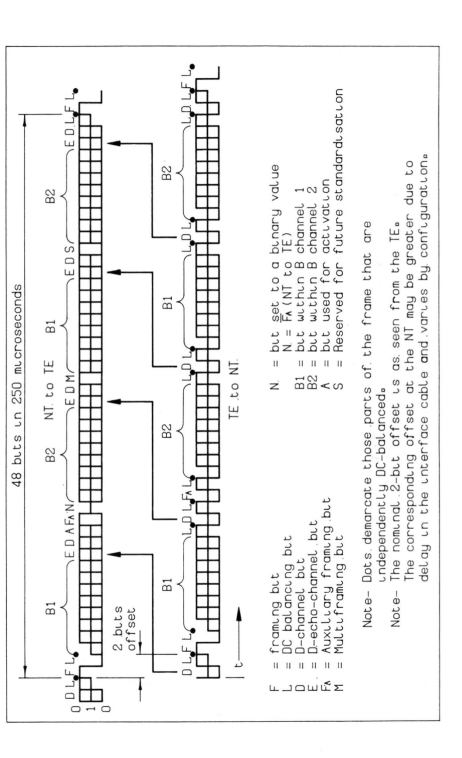

48 bits in 250 microseconds

NT to TE

TE to NT

F = framing bit
L = DC balancing bit
D = D-channel bit
E = D-echo-channel bit
FA = Auxiliary framing bit
M = Multiframing bit

N = bit set to a binary value
N = FA (NT to TE)

B1 = bit within B channel 1
B2 = bit within B channel 2
A = bit used for activation
S = Reserved for future standardisation

Note- Dots demarcate those parts of the frame that are
      independently DC-balanced.
Note- The nominal 2-bit offset is as seen from the TE.
      The corresponding offset at the NT may be greater due to
      delay in the interface cable and varies by configuration.

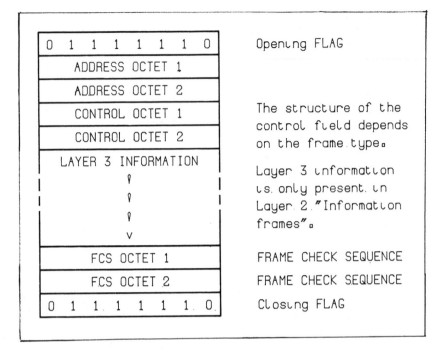

Fig.8.6 - Layer 2 frame structure

Layer 2 multiplexing is achieved by employing a separate layer 2 address for each LAP, the address being made up of the Terminal Endpoint Identifier (TEI) and the Service Access Point Identifier (SAPI). The SAPI identifies the service for which the signalling frame is intended. (For example SAPI 00 = Telephony and SAPI 16 = packet communication). The TEI value is unique to each terminal on a particular installation. The combination of the TEI and the SAPI identify the LAP and provide a unique layer 2 address. A terminal uses this address in all its transmitted frames and only accepts received frames carrying this address.

The control field is one or two octets long depending on the frame type and carries information that identifies the frame and the sequence number for link control. The information element is only present in frames that carry layer 3 information. The Frame Check Sequence is used for error detection.

In order to get an appreciation of the operation of layer 2 consider a terminal as it attempts to establish a call.

If there has been no previous communication it is necessary to establish the interface in a controlled way; a request for service from the customer results in layer 3 requesting a service from layer 2. Layer 2 can not offer a service until layer 1 is ready so layer 2 makes the appropriate request to layer 1 which initiates its start up procedure.

Before layer 2 is ready to offer a service to layer 3 it must initiate the layer 2 start up procedure known as establishing a LAP. This is order to align the state variables that will be used to ensure the correct sequencing of the information frames. Once the LAP is established Layer 2 is able to carry layer 3 information and is said to be in the multiple frame established state. In this state its frame protection mechanism operates.

Once a LAP is established every Information frame (I frame) must be acknowledged by the far end. The most basic response is the Receiver Ready (RR) response frame. The number of frames outstanding before acknowledgement is called the window size and may vary between 1 and 127; the default value for signalling is 1 and for packet information is 7.

The method of recovering from a lost or corrupted frame is based on the use of a timer which is started every time a frame is transmitted, and reset when the appropriate response is received. If the transmitted frame is not acknowledged before the timer expires a retransmission occurs. If after a number of retransmissions, the correct acknowledgement is still not received, layer 2 assumes the link has failed and attempts to re-establish the LAP.

8.4.2 Layer 3

The CCITT layer 3 recommendation I451 describes the procedures necessary for the Call Control. Layer 3 call control information is carried in the information elements of layer 2 frames.

Fig.8.7 shows the layer 3 message sequence for call establishment and clearing.

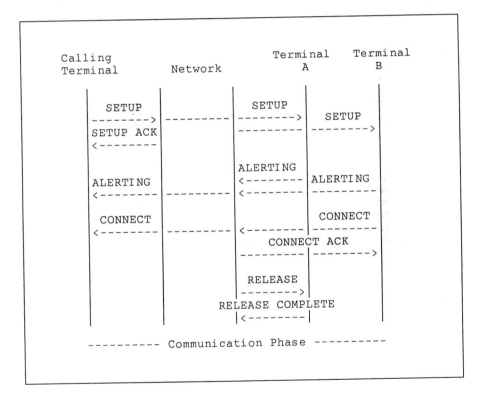

Fig.8.7 - Layer 3 message sequence for call establishment

In order to make an outgoing call the calling terminal must send all the necessary call information (i.e. calling party number and supplementary service request) to the network. The call request must also specify the particular service required for the call (i.e. Speech, 64 kBit/s unrestricted) and any terminal compatibility information.

Following receipt of sufficient information for call establishment signalling information is forwarded across the network using the inter-exchange signalling system CCITT No 7.

At the called side a SETUP message is delivered to the called party via a Broadcast Data Link. All terminals connected can examine the SETUP message to determine whether or not they are compatible with the calling party.

All compatible terminals which are able to accept the call will return an ALERTING message to the network. At the same time, if appropriate, the terminal should give a local indication of the incoming call (i.e. ringing). When a terminal answers it forwards a CONNECT message to the Network. The network will allocate the call to the first terminal to return a CONNECT and will instruct that terminal to connect to the appropriate B channel by returning a CONNECT ACKnowledge containing the B channel information. All other terminals which responded to the call will receive a RELEASE message.

Following the receipt of a CONNECT from the called terminal the network will advise the calling parity that the call has been answered by sending it a CONNECT message. Call charging then commences.

The general structure of layer 3 messages is shown in Fig.8.8.

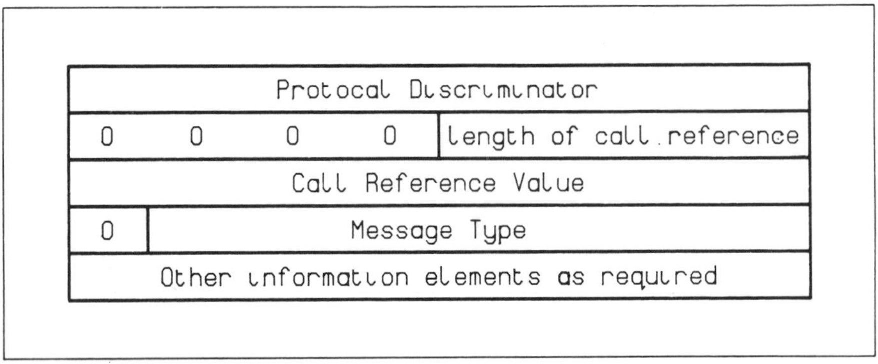

Protocol Discriminator				
0	0	0	0	Length of call reference
Call Reference Value				
0	Message Type			
Other information elements as required				

Fig.8.8 - Layer 3 message structure

The first octet contains a protocol discriminator which gives the D channel the capability of simultaneously supporting additional communication protocols in the future

The call reference in the third octet identifies to which call the message is associated.

The message type code in the forth octet describes the intention of the message (e.g. a "SETUP" message to request call establishment). A number of other information elements may be included following the message type. The content of these elements is dependent on the message type, however the coding rules are open ended and, in principle, it is possible to include additional elements to satisfy any requirement which may be identified in the future.

8.5.   SERVICES

8.5.1 Introduction

There are two main categories of ISDN telecommunication services:

a. Bearer Service: a telecommunication service that provides the capability for the transmission of signals between user-network interfaces.

b. Teleservice: a telecommunication service that provides the complete capability, including terminal equipment functions, for communication between users according to agreed protocols.

The teleservices may then be subdivided into basic services and supplementary services. A basic service is one that can be offered to the customer as a stand alone service and a supplementary Service is a service which modifies or supplements a basic Telecommunication Service (i.e. it cannot be offered as a stand alone service). CCITT work on supplementary services has concentrated on those commonly associated with telephony.

8.5.2 Bearer Services

Bearer services provide the capacity for information transfer and involve only the lower layer functions (layers 1 to 3 of the OSI model). Each bearer service is described by a number of attributes which are intended to be independent. Some of the more important attributes are listed below:

Information transfer mode: describes the operational mode for transferring user information through the ISDN e.g. circuit or packet

Information transfer rate: describes the bit rate for circuit mode bearer services or throughput for packet mode bearer services

Information transfer capability: describes the capability associated with the transfer of different types of information through the ISDN. e.g. Unrestricted digital information (transparent end to end 64 kbit/s B channel suitable for speech or transparent access to a X25 network) or 3.1 kHz audio (transparent end to end 3.1 kHz audio A-law encoded at the user-network interface suitable for voice band data via a modem or speech)

8.5.3 Teleservices

Teleservices provide the full capability for communication by means of terminal and network functions and generally involve both lower and higher (OSI layers 4 to 7) layer functions. Examples of teleservices are Telephony, Teletex and Videotex. The attributes for the ISDN teleservices are grouped into three largely independent categories:
Low layer attributes (as for bearer services)
High layer attributes
General attributes
The high layer attributes specify the type of user information e.g Telephony, Teletex, Facsimile Group 2/3, Facsimile Group 4 and Videotex

8.6. SUPPORT OF EXISTING (NON-ISDN) TERMINALS

8.6.1 Introduction

Clearly for the ISDN to be a success it must support existing non-ISDN terminals at the R reference point. To enable this Terminal Adapter (TA) functions have been specified. The relevant recommendations are:

I.461 Support of X.21 and X.21 bis DTEs

I.462 Support of packet mode terminal equipment

I.463 Support of V-Series type interfaces

8.6.2   Support of X.21 and X.21 bis DTEs

I461 covers TAs for the support of X.21 and X.21 bis Data Terminal Equipment (DTE). The functions to be performed by the TA are:
- rate adaptation: asynchronous data is padded with stop elements.
- signalling conversion: X21 to I-series.
- ready for data alignment, to ensure no user data is lost or that information received by an X21 terminal is erroneously treated as user data.

8.6.3   Support of Packet Mode Terminal Equipment

I462 recognizes that the PSTN and the Packet switched Public Data Network (PSPDN - PSS in the UK) may not merge to become a true ISDN but may remain as separate networks. It addresses the problem of integrating the access procedures to these two separate networks
At the customer end recommendation I420 (basic rate access) covers both circuit and packet switch access, the customer using the same basic procedures to access either type of service/network. It is at the exchange end that the different types of call are separated.
The D channel operates the LAP D protocol which allows both signalling and data packets to be statistically multiplexed across the user-network interface. High speed packet access may be provided on the B Channels (48 or 64 kbit) and low speed access via the D channel (up to 9.6 kbit/s).
Two scenarios are described in I462 for the network handling of packet communication from terminals:

Case A (nee minimum integration), see Fig.8.9.a. The PSPDN service. This matches the method of interworking of BT's pilot service. This scenario connects a packet terminal transparently through the ISDN to the PSPDN. Only access via the B channel is possible.

Case B (nee maximum integration), see Fig.8.9.b. The ISDN virtual Circuit Bearer Service. The packet handling function is within the ISDN and both B and D channel access are supported.

8.6.3.1 PSPDN Service.   For this scenario packet calls are handled transparently through the ISDN, whose only function is to transport 64 kbit/s between the X25 port on the DTE and the Packet Network.
Where access to the PSPDN is by a semi-permanent circuit the TA performs only rate adaptation. For switched access a two stage call set up is required. That is, first the establishment of the ISDN access circuit using LAP D signalling procedures on the D channel followed by the control phase of the virtual circuit using X25 procedures on the B channel. For calls to the DTE the Access Unit in the PSPDN sets up the ISDN link to the terminal before initiating the packet procedures.
Terminals connected to semi-permanent circuits will have a packet network number where-as terminals connected to the switched access will have an ISDN number.

8.6.3.2 ISDN virtual bearer service.   In this scenario the packet handling function is within the ISDN and all terminals have ISDN numbers. Both B and D channel access are supported.
D channel access requires no establishment phase across the ISDN (although the link between the terminal and the exchange must first have been established), it requires only X25 procedures to establish a call. The intention of D channel access is

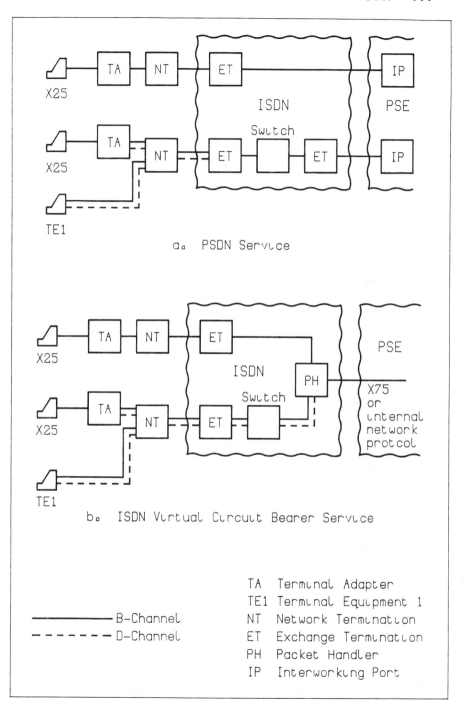

Fig.8.9 - Packet mode terminal access.

to provide each terminal on a user/network interface with what appears to be a dedicated circuit connected to the PSS.

For B channel access there is a two stage call set up as for the PSPDN described previously; that is, the packet call is routed within the ISDN to the packet handler function which processes the call.

In general, the B channel will support a single LAP with multiple packet calls (virtual circuits) achieved by layer 3 multiplexing. The D channel will support multiple links from separate terminals using the Layer 2 multiplexing inherent in LAP D.

8.6.4   Support of V-Series Type Interfaces

I463 describes the terminal adaptor functions necessary to support terminals with interfaces for modems conforming to the V series recommendations on an ISDN. These functions include the conversion of the electrical and mechanical interface characteristics, bit rate adaptation and end-to-end synchronization of the entry to, and the exit from, the data transfer phase. Two types of TA are described, one for manual calling and answering (TA-A) and one for automatic calling and/or answering (TA-B).

8.7.   ISDN DEVELOPMENTS

8.7.1   UK ISDN Pilot service

On the 25th June 1985 BT launched the world's first public IDA service with the objectives of acquiring for BT and its equipment suppliers experience on the technology, development and operational aspects of providing a National ISDN. It also stimulated interest amongst customers and terminal equipment manufacturer's. Because the pilot service was launched prior to the CCITT I-series recommendations it does not conform to those standards but to BT's own interim standards. Nevertheless, the service is still in operation with about 500 in-service lines and it is BT's intention to support it while there remains a demand.

The pilot provides two methods of access to the customer which are marketed as Single line IDA and Multi-Line IDA. These correspond with the I-series basic rate access and primary rate access respectively.

Multi-Line IDA consists of thirty 64 kbit/s channels in a 2 Mbit/s PCM system. This is the same as the CCITT primary rate access except that the common channel signalling system used in timeslot 16 is BT's Digital Access Signalling System 2 (DASS2).

Single line IDA consists of a digital transmission system over the ordinary copper pair to the customers premises.

For the pilot two independent traffic channels are provided over a burst mode transmission system operating at an instantaneous bit rate of 256 kbit/s (giving a maximum operating distance of approximately 2.5 Km over 0.4 mm copper conductors). One channel is at 64 kbit/s and may be used for speech or data, the other channel is at 8 kbit/s and is for data only. An 8 kbit/s common channel signalling channel is also provided.

The pilot network terminating equipment (currently the NTE4) on the customer's premises provides the customer with X21 interfaces for both the 8 and 64 kbit/s traffic channels. Terminal adapters are available to provide other interfaces such as X21 bis/V24. An X21 digital telephone has also been developed.

The Pilot service promoted the development of a number of specialized applications including:

Photo Videotex - A PC based application which retrieves photographic quality colour pictures in around six seconds from a central data base, suitable for picture libraries, travel and estate agents use.

Fast fax - available as the high definition Group 4 standard as well as the Group 3 standard machines.

Slow Scan TV - Enables a new TV picture to be produced every 5 seconds, suitable for surveillance and conferencing applications.

Graphics and Artwork - Applications for use in the publishing and advertising sector, used for colour picture transfers during consulting phases of design and printing process.

BT is to shortly introduce an I-series basic rate access ISDN service which it will market as the IDA National service. For this service an Adaptive Echo Canceller using the line code 3B2T is to be used, which results in a range that gives very nearly 100% penetration.
Initially the service will be provided using ISDN multiplexers and NT1s. Up to 15 of these NT1s may be connected to a multiplexer which in turn is directly connected to the digital local exchange via a 2 Mbit/s link. The 2 Mbit/s link uses the same DASS2 signalling standard as used in the Multi-Line IDA pilot service. This approach has meant:

The digital local exchange will have a consistent interface for all ISDN terminations.

During periods of evolving standards the multiplexer to customer line transmission system can evolve separately from the local exchange.

The equipment can be procured on a competitive basis, independent of the local exchange.

Other plans for the introduction of ISDN by optical fibres are well in hand. BT have introduced Flexible Access Systems (FAS) to customer sites with 25 lines upwards. FAS can handle the Plain Old Telephone Service (POTS), analogue and digital private circuits as well as ISDN.

8.7.2 Developments in Europe

The European Conference of Postal and Telecommunications Administration (CEPT) is responsible for co-ordinating the telecommunications policies of European administrations. Recently CEPT have delegated all its technical ISDN work to ETSI (European Telecommunication Standards Institute).
In late 1986 the European Commission produced a plan for the co-ordinated introduction of ISDN in the EEC member countries. Two important aims were that by 1993 ISDN access would be available to 5% of subscribers lines and that by 1998 ISDN would be accessible to 80% of the population. It is now acknowledged that, in general, these timetables are unlikely to be achieved and that the slip is probably about two years, although plans are obviously well advanced, particularly in France and Germany where a service has been introduced.
The European Commission is pursuing a policy of opening the market for telecommunication terminals and services with the objective of creating a large harmonized home market for European manufacturers which could also provide a platform for world-wide sales. To assist in this in December 1988 CEPT produced a Memorandum of Understanding (MoU) on the implementation of a European ISDN Service by 1992. The purpose of this agreement is to provide a framework for all the necessary measures to be taken to ensure the opening of a commercial European public ISDN services by 1992 providing, amongst other things:

1) Interfaces, i.e.,
    Basic access user-network,
    Primary rate access user-network,
    International
2) Services and supplementary services.

The parties involved in the MoU shall offer a minimum set of services. Offering of the additional services is dependent on the development of the market and will be based on commercial considerations. The parties agree that all services, when offered, will comply with the agreed relevant ETSI standards.
To achieve a Europe-wide market implies interchangeability of terminals i.e. a terminal can be connected to, and operate with, any of the networks without any modification.
To ensure interchangeability, CEPT have produced a series of specifications called NETs (Norme Europeene de Telecommunications). NETs will be used for type approval of terminal equipment and for permission to connect to the relevant networks. NETs have been divided into two general classes:

(i) Access NETs; The terminal function is undefined; only interaction with the particular network is specified.

(ii) Terminal specific NETs; The terminal function is defined

A NET for access functions will ensure that calls can be routed successfully and will prove that the terminal can be connected to the network without the disruption of network operation. Where appropriate, a NET will ensure end-to-end compatibility with the defined telecommunication service.
For a Terminal-Specific NET, additional terminal requirements are specified to ensure effective end-to-end communication.

8.7.3 ISDN Terminals

As field trials and services are becoming available so are ISDN Terminals. These fall broadly into three groups, TAs which permit ISDN access for existing non-ISDN Terminals, ISDN Feature Phones and Communication cards for Personal Computers (PCs). The Feature Phone and the PC Communication card often also include the TA functions, so providing a data port. Another permutation is the combination of a Feature Phone with the PC Communication card so giving an integrated voice and data terminal. This type of terminal would include management facilities which permit, for example, a user to dial voice calls from a personal directory on the computer, to display the incoming caller's name and to dial a number displayed on the computer screen. The computer can also provide a log of all calls and monitor traffic.

The ISDN allows a PC to communicate in much the same way as modems do, but at greatly increased speeds, and the ISDN protocol provides greater capability and functionality to the PC user. One such example is in a PC to host configuration: the PC may act as a remote terminal over a 9.6 kbit/s X25 'D' channel connection while simultaneously transferring data over the B channels at 64 kbit/s.

Many software applications are becoming available to make use of ISDN PC Communication cards ranging from the linking of a video camera to convert the PC into a video-telephone to the conversion of existing LANs into WANs.

8.8. CONCLUSIONS

The world-wide availability of telephony IDNs makes ISDN possible in most developed countries, and the relatively small amount of development work required to enhance the digital exchanges for ISDN provision ensures that the transition to integrated services is already under way. The standardization of the customer's interface has been designed to allow the benefit of world-wide compatibility and portability of ISDN equipment and services. This should produce cost savings through the availability of terminals from many suppliers world-wide. The advantages provided by the ISDN over the telephone network are the increased information capabilities for the customer, the provision of new user-friendly services and the utilization of virtual connections for existing services. These have all been made possible by the introduction of out-of-band signalling.

Many countries have already successfully completed trials and have set up pilot services in their main cities. These have demonstrated the benefits of an ISDN and highlighted the growing interest in the network by customers and terminal manufacturers. Many of the larger telecommunications administrations have introduced ISDN circuit switched services, with nation-wide coverage and integration of other services being introduced from the 1990s. The Integrated Services Digital Network is no longer a concept of the future. Its introduction is well under way internationally, ensuring that the ISDN will become the world-wide all-purpose communications network.

Chapter 9

High Speed Local Area Networks

Prof. Steve R. Wilbur

9.1 INTRODUCTION

Local area networks (LANs) were first developed in the early 1970s, with commercial products appearing in the early 1980s. Such LANs generally operated at data rates between 100 Kb/s and 10 Mb/s over distances of a few kilometres. These might be termed *First Generation LANs*, have now been supported commercially for several years, and have an industry or international standard specification. The most common of these, which will be discussed briefly below, is the ISO 8802/3 CSMA/CD (Carrier Sense Multiple Access with Collision Detection) bus structured LAN [8802/3]. Although the term *Ethernet* actually describes a proprietary standard developed by DEC, Intel and Xerox which differs slightly from the ISO standard, it is often colloquially used for any CSMA/CD LAN. Many professional workstations are now sold with Ethernet interfaces as standard, allowing them to work in a distributed computing environment sharing filing and printing services.

Experience seems to show that the Ethernet 10 Mb/s capacity is able to support about 10 discless workstations working into a shared fileserver, or up to about 30 with their own local discs. The difference relates to the volume of fileserver traffic, dominated by swapping and program loading in the discless workstation case. Thus, it can be seen that even a medium sized organization or department may need several interconnected LANs. Such interconnection is usually via *bridges* which filter the traffic, so that traffic local to a given LAN does not flow through the bridge to congest another LAN. With care at the planning stage, the *Principle of Locality* applies, ie. a large proportion of traffic is local and only a small proportion goes via bridges to other LANs. For this reason, a *backbone* structure is often favoured where one LAN forms the main inter-LAN trunk, and the others, with user machines attached, form spurs to it via bridges. Even so, with applications such as image processing, or large organizations a 10 Mb/s backbone may frequently become congested.

Partly in response to this need for backbone inter-connection, and partly in an attempt to use LAN technology to deal with voice switching, several higher speed LANs (HSLANs) have been developed. These we might term *Second Generation LANs* . They typically operate in the 50 Mb/s to 150 Mb/s region, over distances of up to 100 Km. The large distances which are now possible are brought about by the use of optical fibre, but in turn it allows new applications to be considered. For example, PTTs have been investigating the feasibility of such networks for providing high speed data services for customers within a city, the so-called *Metropolitan Area Networks (MANs)* , or even linking company offices over a large geographical area [Mollenauer 88]. Second generation LAN products are just becoming available, and the relevant standards are being worked on.

The above justification for first and second generation LANs has been broadly based on the needs for data transmission in connection with computational processes. While the need for this will continue to rise, the integration of communications services into the workstation will place additional demands on the communication infrastructure. Considerable research is underway to investigate the technology, user interfaces, and benefits of integrated voice, image (including video), and data for a variety of industrial applications. For certain types of design discussions, data rates of 50 to 100 Mb/s between user workstations are expected to occur over long periods. Clearly, second generation LANs will be of limited use with such scenarios. *Third Generation LANs* are currently in the research stage. They can probably be characterized as having a data rate in excess of 500 Mb/s (typically 1 Gb/s), and will certainly be capable of carrying circuit traffic such as voice and video, as well as high bit rate data.

This chapter concentrates on the two second generation LANs which are the subject of international standards. In order to understand these, a brief overview of the important principles of first generation LANs is given, together with an outline of the new requirements. Other high speed LANs have been developed, but have not yet become the subject of standards.

9.2   LAN PRINCIPLES

In this section key principles of LANs will be examined. For readers unfamiliar with the technology they are referred to one of the many books on Local Area Networks of which Stallings [Stallings 87] is a good example. An overview can also be found in [Wilbur 86] or [Stallings 84].

9.2.1 CSMA/CD

In CSMA/CD networks all nodes are attached to a single, serial, passive communications bus. Nodes can listen to the bus to determine if data is flowing, and they can transmit to it. Let us suppose that three nodes, A, B, and C are attached as shown in Figure 9.1.

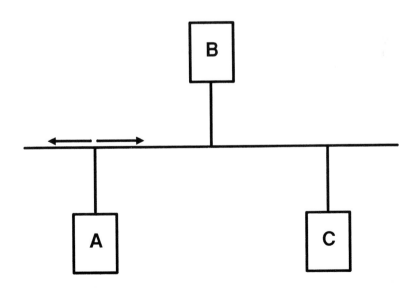

Fig.9.1 - CSMA/CD Principles

If A wishes to transmit to B it first listens until the bus is idle and then begins to transmit. The signal travels in both directions from A, being completely absorbed by the terminators at each end. As it passes another node, eg. B, that node can copy it into local buffers if the transmitted packet's destination matches the node's address. Let us now assume that as the signal nears C, C observing an idle bus up to this point, decides to transmit too. Shortly afterwards there will be a *collision* and the data in the packets from A and C will interfere. C will detect this almost immediately and could stop transmitting, but although A's packet will have been damaged, A will not know about it until the fragment of C's packet has traveled along the cable to A. Thus, the worst case time taken for a collision to be detected occurs when A and C are at extreme ends of the bus, and is equal to twice the propagation time of an electrical signal over the bus length. This parameter is known as the *slot time (S)* and is important in bus LANs using contention protocols.

At time S/2 after transmission has begun all nodes are aware that the bus is busy and will not attempt to transmit. Thus, S corresponds to the time taken for any node to be assured that it has transmitted the smallest possible packet without collision; anything smaller is assumed to be a collision fragment and is discarded. For an ISO 8802/3 LAN the slot time is 51.2 Ês giving a minimum data size of 46 octets. For a LAN operating at D b/s over distance L metres, the minimum packet size (P) is given by:

$$P = D \times S \qquad \qquad ...(1)$$

and

$$S = k \times c \times L \qquad \qquad ... (2)$$

where c is the speed of light and k is a constant related to the cable properties. Thus,

$$P = k' \times D \times L \qquad \qquad ... (3)$$

Experience shows that the majority of packets on LANs carry between one and 64 octets of user data. By the time protocol headers are included, the 46 octet choice of ISO 8802/3 seems about right as a minimum. It also allows 10 Mb/s LANs spanning about 2.5 Km to be constructed from several segments connected by repeaters. (Segment size is constrained by the ability to detect collisions and is typically 180 - 500 m depending on the medium.)

The importance of equation (3) is that if P is kept at about 50 octets and the data rate is increased, then the maximum LAN length must decrease correspondingly. If CSMA/CD technology is to be used for high speeds then either the minimum packet length must increase or the distance covered must decrease. One of the first high speed LANs, Hyper-Channel, did use the CSMA principle and operated at 50 Mb/s. However, it was intended for inter-connecting mainframes in a computer room, so the distance limitation was not important.

Another problem with the bus technology at higher speeds and distances is that fibre optic cable is essentially a point-to-point medium. Fused optical couplers are apparently difficult to manufacture for greater than about 16 fibres, so cyclic control mechanisms rather than broadcast mechanisms are favoured for fibre LANs.

9.2.2 Slotted Ring

Ring-based LANs are formed by cyclically connecting successive nodes. Thus, each node drives only one link and there is only one receiver at the end. This makes the design of the line drivers much easier than in bus networks where a transmitter may need to drive up to 100 nodes and high amplitude signals may be caused by collisions. As we have already seen, cable introduces a delay, and a figure of 5 ns/m is fairly typical. Nodes also introduce a delay and a minimum figure is about 3 bits. Thus, if we take a ring with 200 m of cable and 10 nodes, the delay in the ring is 40 bit times at 10 Mb/s (10 due to the cable and 30 for the nodes). Another way of looking at this is as a circulating shift register, since a bit injected at one node will return 40 bit times later.

The slotted ring (often called the Cambridge Ring) formats this shift register into one or more *slots* . Each slot contains a full/empty bit, destination and source address fields, and the data together with some housekeeping bits. The total slot length is less than the length of the ring, (38 bits in the case of the original Cambridge ring,) and any spare bits are set to zero and are termed the *gap* . Where there are several slots on a ring, they occur nose-to-tail with a single gap per cycle. A node wishing to transmit data will wait for the next slot to appear, observe the full/empty bit, and if empty will fill the slot with its data. As the full slot passes round the ring each node will inspect it and if full and appropriately addressed it will copy it into local buffers. Meanwhile, the slot continues round the ring and on arriving back at the source it will be marked empty again and passed to the next downstream node for possible use.

It is noteworthy that access to the ring is fair, since a round-robin scheme is used to pass on access to a slot once it has been used. Thus for any given configuration it is possible to predict the maximum data rate which a pair of nodes can sustain. Also, because the slot travels a complete circuit before being re-used, *response bits* are included in each slot so the recipient can mark them to indicate whether the data was accepted or it was busy.

Each slot only carries 16 bits of data in the Cambridge Ring. The round-robin control mechanism ensures that a slot cannot be re-used immediately on return, and the logic has a recovery time which means that only every 1/(N+2) slots can be used by a given node, where N is the number of slots in the ring. A given node can therefore only transmit at a data rate of:

$$D = (16/38) \times 1/(N+2) \qquad \qquad ... (4)$$

giving a maximum node-to-node data rate of about 1.3 Mb/s for a single slot ring. However, the medium is being multiplexed between the several transmitting nodes which gives very low access times to those wishing to transmit a few bytes of data; they are not delayed by ones transmitting kilobytes.

If we increase the transmission rate on the ring the shift register contains more bits, and we can either choose to have more slots, larger slots or a combination. In the Cambridge Fast Ring which operates at 70 Mb/s they have chosen to have 32 octets of data per slot, and 16-bit address fields. This allows more of the capacity to be used by individual nodes and can be valuable for fast devices such as file servers. For a one slot ring with round robin scheduling, two nodes may be simultaneously transmitting at 28 Mb/s, ie. 80% of the ring capacity is being used for data compared to 40% for the slow ring.

As data rates and distances increase, the cost of the slot's wasted return trip before being freed becomes increasingly significant. Where real full duplex traffic exists, (eg. video phone,) it could be used to carry the reverse traffic. However, most traffic is not truly full duplex so releasing the slot at the destination could provide an effective doubling of capacity, albeit with the loss of the response bits.

9.2.3 Token Ring

The token ring also has cyclically inter-connected nodes. In its idle state a token continuously circulates. A node with data to transmit *captures* the token and transmits the data in a packet. Capturing may mean complete removal of the token or merely alteration of one or more bits to form what is sometimes termed a *connector* . Having captured the token the node may be limited to only sending one packet or may be allowed to send several packets before some limit timer expires, depending on the type of token ring. Typically, the recipient can set response bits, and the packet fully returns to the sender before the token is released for other nodes' use.

In some token rings [8802/5] there are a number of priority levels for packets. These work as follows. The transmitting node places its current priority level in the connector, and as this goes round the ring other nodes with more urgent data can over-write this with a higher priority reservation. If the connector returns to the sender with a higher priority bid, it releases the token with the reserved priority after its present packet transmission. Only nodes with data at that priority may capture the token and transmit. Eventually, the token will return to the original sender which is then responsible for reducing the token's priority to its original level. Such a scheme can be nested for several priority levels.

The token ring is generally considered to be one of the best LAN structures in terms of throughput. Being deterministic means that there is no bandwidth wasted on collisions. Since packets are generally of sizes up to a few thousand octets the proportion of the bandwidth used for address and other control purposes is small. Similarly, data is delivered in large chunks without the need for fragmentation and re-assembly as for the slotted ring. Its main drawback is that the delay in accessing the ring for a given node is the sum of the service times of all the upstream nodes. Because packet sizes can be much longer than with the slotted ring, so can the delays. With a mixture of short and long packets to be transmitted the slotted ring would give better performance to the short packets because they would be inter-leaved earlier with the inherent time-division multiplexing of that ring. However, the token ring priority schemes do go some way to reducing this problem for certain classes of traffic.

It was mentioned that, in many cases, the outgoing packet fully returns to the sender before the token is released. With short rings at low data rates this does not significantly consume bandwidth, since the ring delay may be only a few tens of bits. However, as speeds and distances increase the delay will be significant. For example, a 1 Km ring will have a delay of about 5 μs (500 bits at 100 Mb/s), while 100 Km, which is the expected circumference of some Metropolitan Area Networks, would have a delay of 500 μs or about 50,000 bits of delay. Thus, as token rings move to higher speeds *early token release* is used, where the sender appends the token immediately after their transmitted packet(s). The benefits of response bits still exist because the packet(s) still return to the sender, but the ring is made available to other nodes much earlier.

However, with early token release in long rings the packet (or connector) may not have fully circulated before the token is passed on so the priority scheme above cannot be used. Instead, priority in these cases is usually based on the observed *token rotation time (TRT)*. If the LAN is unloaded the token will rotate very rapidly, with the rotation time increasing as load builds up. Nodes compare the actual rotation time with the *target token rotation time (TTRT)* for each priority and hold back data for lower priorities when the token is rotating too slowly.

The limiting factor in token ring efficiency is determined by the delay between release of the token at one node and capture at the next downstream node (let us call it the *token slack time*). This time cannot be recovered, it must always be wasted. For high speed rings where the nodes may be separated by a kilometre or more, this delay (about 500 bits, see above) is the size of a small packet such as might be used for interrogation of file servers, or the transport of voice.

9.3   APPLICATIONS AND REQUIREMENTS

The impetus for high speed LANs has come from several quarters. First, is the intellectual curiosity; how fast and large can LANs be made with a given level of technology, and what are the implications for media access control (MAC) protocols? The inverse of this is the technology push which comes from the rapid development and decreasing cost of high performance fibre-optics, and the maturity of VLSI techniques.

However, the other drives come more from applications. We have already seen that first generation LANs provide useful local distribution, but that their capacity is limited even with careful structuring. This is especially true if a solution with file servers on the backbone is favoured. High speed LANs are valuable in this situation. The main requirements are for greater bandwidth and for LAN circumferences which cover a site, probably less than 10 Km. A further requirement is to be able to fragment and inter-connect such HSLANs as the organization's needs grow. Some HSLANs, such as the Cambridge Fast Ring [Hopper 86], include such bridging as part of the design, perhaps to encourage the use of relatively small, manageable backbones, albeit with high inter-ring throughput.

In many countries the boundary of a LAN is the public road. The PTT provides services between buildings of organizations separated in this way, and such services may be switched at up to 64 Kb/s or point-to-point links at higher rates (currently usually up to 2 Mb/s). This discontinuity in data rates and technology means that LANs in separated buildings have to be bridged via slow links rather than being integrated with the company backbone. If PTTs were to provide uncommitted optical fibres to customers, the HSLAN could be extended to outlying sites, but at present such services seem to be unavailable. The HSLAN standards cover circumferences up to 50 or 100 Km so could be used for such purposes if the medium were available.

Related to this is the need of organizations to transfer data at high speed or in large quantities or both to a number of other companies. In other words they would like a high speed switched service often covering a modest area such as an industrial estate or a city. A Metropolitan Area Network would typically be operated by a PTT and serve a number of companies to provide a district backbone. Operationally, this is very different to a LAN, not least because the operator will want to charge for use and the users will require guarantees that their data is not accessible to competitors. However, it has similar architectural requirements to the company backbone.

During the same period that HSLANs have been developed there has been strong emphasis towards the integration of communications services. The ISDN will provide a switched 64 Kb/s service (basic rate ISDN). Primary rate ISDN (2.048 Mb/s) and Broadband ISDN (140 Mb/s) services are, or will soon be available as point-to-point services. Primary rate services are widely used at present for linking PABXs, possibly with some of the 30 64 Kb/s circuits being used for data. The obvious question is whether such circuits could be integrated with data distribution via LANs or HSLANs. Such a facility requires a continuous bit stream to be conveyed from one node to another with only limited variation in the inter-arrival time of the fragments of the stream. Too great a delay of a fragment may mean that a speech or video sample has to be discarded resulting in distortion or apparent noise for the receiver. We shall see below that the transport of such *isochronous* (or circuit) data is included in the specification of the standard HSLANs. Although the slotted ring or token ring can provide suitable guarantees for a given ring configuration, other control strategies are necessary if it is to be configuration independent. The slotted ring is somewhat more appropriate than a token ring for this type of service and a variation based on dynamic load measurement and bandwidth management has been developed for switching isochronous traffic.

Finally, there is a requirement for robustness. A single failure in a backbone must not stop the organization's data communication, neither should the addition of new nodes. The same considerations also apply to MANs. Whilst carefully chosen wiring centres will help to reduce the downtime when a failure occurs, the usual approach is to use a form of duplex network arranged in a ring, so that when a fault is detected the ends can be joined to form a single larger "sausage-shaped" ring. It is usually assumed that the chance of simultaneous failures is very small and that addition or removal of nodes can be scheduled sequentially. Thus the ability to recover from a single fault is normally adequate.

9.4   FIBRE DISTRIBUTED DATA INTERFACE (FDDI)

The Fibre Distributed Data Interface (FDDI) began life within the ANSI standards body as a form of network suitable for the interconnection of mainframes and their high speed peripherals, or as a backbone for first generation LANs. An enhancement, known as FDDI-II, was developed to address circuit switching. FDDI has now been adopted by ISO, and with the exception of the station management functions, the component standards have reached at least Draft International Standard (DIS) status. However, the term FDDI-II has been dropped in favour of *hybrid ring control (HRC)* and those provisions should be balloted shortly.

FDDI is basically a token ring with early token release. It consists of two counter-rotating optical fibre rings. The standards are organized into three layers: physical media dependent (PMD), physical (PHY), and media access control (MAC). The existing ISO LLC protocols are expected to sit above these layers. A management standard (SMT) is now generally stable, but is unlikely to be balloted before the end of 1989. The draft standards are in [FDDI 86, 87, 88a, 88b] although more recent versions exist in most cases. There are now production VLSI chip-sets available which implement FDDI, and others are expected this year.

9.4.1 Physical Medium Dependent (PMD)

The optical fibre infrastructure of FDDI consists of a pair of fibres for the link between two nodes. These are terminated in a special polarized connector so that the primary and secondary ring are identified. LEDs operating at 1300 nm are used to transmit the light and PIN diodes are used as receptors. A limit of 2 Km per link is imposed by the standard, and this is limited by the chromatic dispersion of the LED. The relevant committee is investigating the possible use of single mode fibres over link distances of up to 50 Km. The recommended fibre has a core diameter of 62.5 µm and a cladding of 125 µm. Use of other fibres, in particular the popular 50/125 µm type, will likely be allowed in future, provided the link power budget of 11 dB can be met, even under fold-back conditions.

There are two types of nodes, single and dual. The dual nodes can attach directly to the ring, while single nodes attach via a concentrator. Dual nodes and concentrators may have by-pass facilities as shown in Figure 9.2.

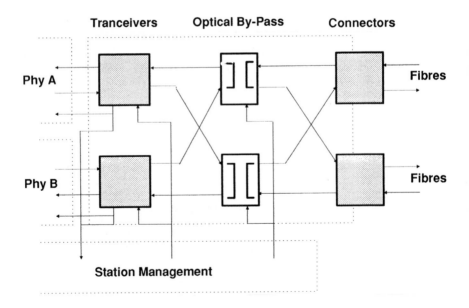

Fig.9.2 - FDDI Optical By-Pass

Without a node attached the by-pass is in the position shown so that the primary ring input is connected to the primary output, and similarly for the secondary. The PHY side of the by-pass is connected similarly allowing nodes to self-test almost to the fibre plant. When tests are satisfactory, the switch connects the PHY signals to the physical ring. The optical switch is in fact mechanical, the control current being used to switch the alignment of the optical signals. Note that the signal arrangements at the PHY interface is identical to that at the fibre connectors. Thus, the optical by-pass can be omitted in cheaper products. Loop-back under fault conditions is controlled by SMT and performed at the MAC layer.

9.4.2 Physical Layer (PHY)

The PHY layer functions provide the remainder of the physical layer facilities. Data on the ring is transmitted at 125 MHz although a 4/5 coding reduces the data rate to 100 Mb/s. Clocks are regenerated and synchronized at each node via elasticity buffers and the size of these limits the packet size to 4500 octets.
Data is transmitted on the fibres as 5 bit symbols with certain symbols (violations or V symbols) being disallowed because they would violate engineering considerations for clock recovery. 16 of the possible 32 states are used to transmit data, with a further 8 being used for control and signalling purposes. These are shown below:

Line State:	Q	Quiet
	I	Idle
	H	Halt
Start Delimiter:	J	First of pair
	K	Second of Pair
End Delimiter:	T	Terminator
Control:	R	Reset
	S	Set

9.4.3 Media Access Control

The FDDI standard assumes a maximum total wiring distance of 100 Km, which means a total fibre path of up to 200 Km under wrapped conditions. It also allows up to 500 nodes to be attached.
The token and packet (frame) structures are shown in Figure 9.3.

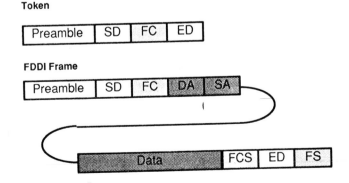

Fig.9.3 - FDDI Token and Frame Structure.

All frames are preceded by a preamble which consists of Idle symbols (I) and is used for clock synchronization, a Starting Delimiter (JK pair), and a Frame Control field. The frame control field consist of 8 bits which convey information such as whether this is a token, MAC frame, LLC frame or management frame, the type of management frame, and for other than the token, whether 16 or 48 bit addressing is being used for this frame.

A frame containing data will then be followed by the destination address, source address, data and frame check sequence. Following these is an End Delimiter, which is one or more T symbols. Finally, for data frames there are a minimum of 3 symbols corresponding to the Frame Status which must be R or S values. These are the response bits and indicate error detected, address recognized and frame copied. Implementors may define additional indicators in this field, but they can only be set to R or S values.

FDDI operates in two modes: *asynchronous* and *synchronous* (not to be confused with the isochronous mode with hybrid ring control). Asynchronous working is the normal token ring mode and dynamically allocates any bandwidth remaining after the synchronous requirements have been met. The synchronous mode is for applications which have a predictable requirement where predictable response is needed. A target token rotation time is agreed by all nodes at ring initialization and the token rotation time is monitored during operation. If the token returns earlier than TTRT the node can send either synchronous or asynchronous traffic; if it returns later, only synchronous traffic is allowed. Synchronous mode is managed by the station management (SMT) layer which arbitrates bids for bandwidth such that the sum of the allocations, the time for a maximum length packet, and a token circulation must not exceed TTRT. Because each node is allowed to transmit synchronous frames up to TTRT-TRT in duration or its allocation, whichever is the greater, the TRT will sometimes exceed TTRT, but it will always be less than 2 x TTRT.

Asynchronous mode has two forms: *non-restricted* and *restricted* tokens. Non-restricted tokens are the norm, and allow even sharing of the bandwidth between nodes. A priority scheme can be used, which is also based on the token rotation time. For those occasions when a pair or group of nodes wish to use all the available asynchronous bandwidth the token can be restricted. Higher level protocols are used to establish which nodes are involved in the dialogue, and during this one of them issues a restricted token. This can only be used by the closed group, and prevents other non-restricted tokens and transmissions (including management functions) for the dialogue duration. Eventually, the issuer will re-issue a non-restricted token to return the ring to normal operation. The FDDI network is always initialized to a non-restricted token.

Initialization of the ring achieves two things. One is to ensure that only one token is circulating and the other is to agree a TTRT among all nodes. It is performed when one or more nodes discovers inactivity or incorrect activity on the ring, usually an over-long period before arrival of the token. The node then continuously transmits Claim Frame s containing its bid for TTRT together with its address. Received claims are examined and the node stops transmitting using the following criteria:

a. it cedes to claims with lower TTRT,

b. For equal TTRT, it cedes to those with longer address (48 bits vs 16),

c. For equal address length, the highest address wins.

Eventually one node will receive its own claims back and it then has responsibility for propagating the agreed TTRT and injecting the token. The first token cycle allows all stations to synchronize, the second allows synchronous transmission and after that full operation begins.

Some of the functions above are managed by the SMT functions. Other functions handle ring breaks and wrap-around as well as the *beaconing* process which notifies downstream nodes of a significant fault and can be used by operations staff to localize faults.

9.4.4 Hybrid Ring Control (FDDI-II)

Hybrid ring control (HRC) was originally termed FDDI-II by the ANSI committee. This description is based on that earlier ANSI X3T9 work so the term FDDI-II will be used, although HRC is now being worked on by the standards group.

The differences between synchronous and isochronous mode are: with synchronous mode data must be sent in large bursts whereas with isochronous transmission a steady flow of smaller data units is achieved. Synchronous mode provides a bound on the transit delay, but the actual delay may vary widely within the limit depending on the actual instantaneous load. With isochronous forms the delay is virtually constant.

FDDI-II mode is begun by one node negotiating the right to become cycle master on a ring operating in token mode. This node then has the responsibility for generating an integral number of 125 μs cycles (slots) round the ring and any padding to accommodate them. The cycles are synchronized to an 8 KHz clock source, eg. that used in telephone systems. Figure 9.4 shows the format of a cycle.

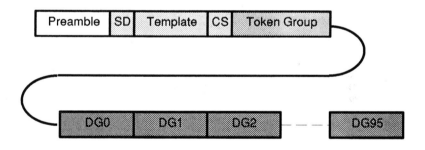

Fig.9.4 - FDDI-II Cycle Structure.

The preamble is provided for synchronization of the 125 MHz node clocks and the SD is the usual JK sequence. The main part of the cycle is the 96 data groups, each containing 16 octets of data. Essentially, these provide 16 circuit switched channels operating at 6.144 Mb/s (3 x 2.048 Mb/s or 4 x 1.538 Mb/s) leaving about 2 Mb/s of the LAN capacity for control and asynchronous operation. The 16 circuits are controlled by the 16 symbols in the template which indicate whether they are in use for circuit data or are free. Thus, circuit N is made up of 96 octets, one from each data group. The 16 octet token group field and any unused channels in the data group are used to provide residual token ring (asynchronous) facilities. The format of the token ring is similar to that of standard FDDI except that the start delimiter is replaced by Halt and Idle symbols to prevent confusion with the SD of the FDDI-II cycles.

Allocation or release of circuits is done by the cycle master, and to prevent disruption to the asynchronous token activities, it captures the token before changing the template.

9.5   IEEE 802.6 METROPOLITAN AREA NETWORK

There has been an IEEE 802.6 activity looking into metropolitan area networks for some while. Originally it focused on token rings operating at rates up to 20 Mb/s. Recently, the submission of a LAN architecture called QPSX (Queued Packet and Synchronous Switch) from Australia has re-vitalized D the activity, and the IEEE MAN work is now based on QPSX. Because QPSX is also the name of a company marketing this technology, the network is now known as a Distributed Queue Dual Bus (DQDB) network. The form of the network is very different from those above [Newman 88] and the standards work is at a early stage [IEEE 802.6] so the remainder of the chapter will concentrate on the principles with a brief look at the salient points of the standard.

9.5.1 Principles

As shown in Figure 9.5, the network consists of two uni-directional, serial buses A and B.

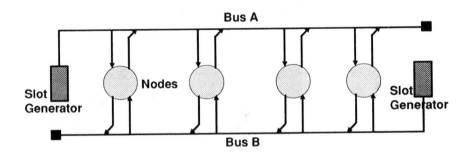

Fig.9.5 - DQDB Structure.

The operation of DQDB is symmetric with respect to both these buses, so we shall concentrate on the transmission of data along the A bus. Transmission along the B bus is identical other than interchanging A and B in this description. At the head of each bus is a slot generator and both generate slots at the same rate. Slots are completely absorbed at the tail of each bus. All nodes are connected to both buses and they can read the passing traffic and over-write it as needed. They cannot remove data, though.

Although logically a bus structure, physically DQDB is a ring. The ring is broken at the node providing the slot generators, as shown in Figure 9.6.

Co-Located Slot Generators

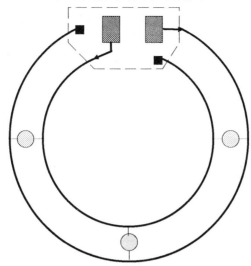

Fig.9.6 - DQDB Slot Generation.

The slot generators are expected to be synchronized to the 8 Khz PTT reference frequency so if there should be a break in the cable the nodes either side can act as slot generators and still be synchronized. The management functions arrange for the slot generation functions to migrate automatically to the site of the failure. It is intended to operate at data rates of about 150 Mb/s over distances of the order of 100 Km, using optical fibres as the medium.

DQDB provides a perfect queuing structure. The elements of the reservation protocol are shown in Figure 9.7.

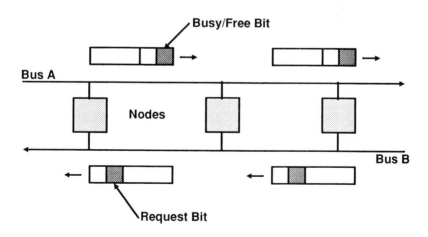

Fig.9.7 - DBDQ Principles.

Each slot has a full/empty bit and a request bit together with a data transport field. Each time a slot passes upstream with a request bit set the node's request queue is incremented. If the node wishes to transmit it must continue incrementing the queue as requests pass upstream, until a slot without a request arrives. It can now insert its request, and add itself into its queue. Other requests continue to arrive, so there are two elements of the queue: the number of requests before the node's own, and the number after. (At any time nodes can only have one of their own requests outstanding.) As empty slots arrive these are passed downstream to honour earlier requests and the node's queue is decremented. When the counter reaches zero, the node can transmit its data. Clearly, if the request queue is empty when a node wants to transmit it uses the next free slot after sending a request.

It is straightforward to extend this scheme to allow several priority levels. There needs to be one bit in each slot corresponding to a request at a given level and a similar number of queues in each node. As slots pass downstream the highest priority non-empty queue in each node is decremented.

With DQDB, all nodes are provided an opportunity to transmit based on the time at which they were able to access a request bit in an upstream slot. This scheme does not suffer problems similar to token slack time, because slots can, in principle, be transmitted nose-to-tail. By keeping the slots of fixed, short length the latency for access is kept low, rather like the slotted ring, at the small cost of fragmentation and re-assembly being needed for large transfers. There is no notion of response bits with DQDB, since the ring is not closed.

9.5.2 The Standards Work

The work on this standard is still in progress, so the following information is tentative, being taken from an early unapproved draft. Operating parameters are only defined to be greater than 1 Mb/s and 50 Km diameter.

Two types of slots are being proposed: *queued-arbitrated (QA)* to transfer asynchronous data, and *non-arbitrated (NA)* to transfer isochronous data. The QA slots are controlled in the way described above. The NA slots are generated by the slot generator at a rate sufficient to satisfy the demands for circuit switched traffic, and nodes are allowed to read and write only agreed portions of such slots, very much like the data groups of FDDI-II. One difference is that NA slots contain an identifier (VCI) which a node can examine to see if the slot relates to its circuits.

A slot consists of an *access control field (ACF)* of one octet followed by a segment containing 68 data octets. The ACF contains two bits to indicate one of: NA slot, busy QA slot, or empty QA slot. It also contains four bits which can be set to indicate a request at one of the four priority levels. Both QA and NA segments consist of a four octet header followed by 64 octets of data. The header contains a VCI, data type indication, and priority indication as well as a check sequence.

The asynchronous MAC layer is carried over QA slots. A MAC frame consists of a header, between 3 and 9188 octets of data and a trailing check sequence. The header structure is fixed format and contains address fields, protocol identification, quality of service indication, bridging indication, a length indicator and a check sequence. Addresses may be 16, 48 or 60 bits in length and 64 bits are used for each address including a type field and the necessary padding. The 60 bit addresses may be either publicly or privately administered; the public addresses will conform to CCITT address norms. The protocol identifier field has only one value reserved being 1 for LLC. Quality of service includes the ability to indicate one of 4 levels for each of delay and packet loss. The bridging indication is for further study, and the length field specifies the total length of the MAC frame (max. 9216).

This frame structure is segmented and sent via QA slots, with the 64 octet slots being split into a two octet header and the 62 octets of the frame. The header indicates first, last and intermediate slots of a frame, and also contains the sequence number.

9.6 REFERENCES

[8802/3]   "CSMA/CD Local Area Networks", ISO IS 8802.3

[8802/5]   "Token Ring Local Area Networks", ISO DIS 8802/5

[Burr 86]   Burr WE, "The FDDI Optical Data Link", IEEE Communications Magazine, Vol 24, No 5, pp 18-23, May 1986

[FDDI 86]   "FDDI Station Management (SMT)", ANSI X3T9.5/84-49, Draft September 1986

[FDDI 87]   "Fiber Distributed Data Interface Physical Layer Media Dependent (PMD)", ISO/DP 9314/3, August 1987

[FDDI 88a]   "Fibre Distributed Data Interface (FDDI) - Part 1: Physical Layer Protocol (PHY)", ISO DIS 9314-1, January 1988

[FDDI 88b]   "Fibre Distributed Data Interface (FDDI) - Part 2: Media Access Control (MAC)", ISO DIS 9314-2, January 1988

[Hopper 86]   Hopper A, Needham RM, "The Cambridge Fast Ring Networking System (CFR)", University of Cambridge Computer Laboratory Tech. Report 90, June 1986

[IEEE 802.6]   "Proposed Standard Distributed Queue Dual Bus (DQDB) Metropolitan Area Network (MAN)", IEEE P802.6/D6, Unapproved Draft, November 1988

[Mollenauer 88]   Mollenauer JF, "Standards for Metropolitan Area Networks", IEEE Communications Magazine, Vol 26, No 4, pp 15-19, April 1988

[Newman 88]   Newman RM, Budrikis ZL, Hullett JL, "The QPSX Man", IEEE Communications Magazine, Vol 26, No 4, pp 20-28, April 1988

[Ross 86]   Ross FE, "FDDI - A Tutorial", IEEE Communications Magazine, Vol 24, No 5, pp 10-17, May 1986

[Stallings 87]   Stallings W, "Local Networks: An Introduction", Macmillan, ISBN 0-02-415520-9,1987

[Stallings 84]   Stallings W, "Local Networks", ACM Computing Surveys, Vol 16, No 1, March 1984

[Wilbur 86]   Wilbur SR, "Local Area Networks" in "Data Communications and Networks" ed. RL Brewster, Peter Peregrinus 1986, ISBN 0-86341-078-2

Chapter 10

Systems Management Architecture

Tony Gale

10.1 GENERAL INTRODUCTION

10.1.1 Scope and Objectives

The Systems Management Architecture described in this chapter is an evolutionary development of the Community Management Architecture which has been developing within ICL since 1982. Evolutionary though it is, this chapter represents a key milestone in that process because it has imported some significant developments from outside ICL and it reflects a more comprehensive understanding of the subject.

The objectives of the Architecture are:

i) To decompose the potentially complex systems for managing a distributed IT system into well defined modules which can be developed and integrated in a flexible manner.

ii) To identify components which are useful in their own right as well as integrable into a Total System.

iii) To incorporate key aspects of the OSI Management Framework to make our offerings Open in an Open Systems World.

iv) To indicate what type and how much investment needs to be made ro realise management of a Total System.

v) To define interfaces and protocols which are the basis of our ability to integrate a Total Systems Management solution.

The major imported developments are:

a) Object Oriented approach to defining managed Objects (OSI standards).

b) Structure of Management Doman (developed by STC plc and accepted by OSI NM.

c) Service Level Agreements as a way of measuring service provided (General development in the IT industry).

10.2 ARCHITECTURAL FRAMEWORK

10.2.1 Basis

The framework and the chosen Architecture are based on a number of important concepts:

a)   General Management Theory: The Systems Management apporoaches must dovetail into the chosen management approaches of our customers; it is, therefore, imperative that there is synergy between the management styles implemented in our products and the style they adopt for their business as a whole.

b)   Object Oriented Approaches: Early developments in Systems Management externally and internally have been based on choosing an appropriate protocol. Although the protocol is important, it is now recognised that an agreed, common model of what is being managed is of paramount importance; the IT community lead by ISO and helped by the OSI NM FORUM is generally adopting the Object Oriented approach to defining these agreed models.

c)   Reuse: Investment in Systems Management is expensive and can be compared with the earlier investments made by the IT industry in Operating Systems. The Architecture must have a prominent position for reuseable components in its basic framework to avoid re-invention and maximise exploitation.

d)   Total Systems Scope: The term "Community Management" was coined in 1983 to demonstrate that the scope was much wider than the more generally used term "Network Management". The IT industry is beginning to recognise this increased scope and using the term "Systems Management" to encompass more than just the network.

Thus the key elements in the Architectural Framework are:

i)   Managed Objects which may be Physical or Logical - so long as an Agent exists to present a coherent managed object model to the outside world.

ii)   Object - Object relationships which are the basis of a integrated system.

iii)   Domains of Management which are characterised by the object types handled within that domain.

iv)   Management Functions, which are replicated in each domain, monitoring and controlling the managed objects.

v)   Management Infrastructure that supports relationships between Functions
and   Objects within the domain.

vi)   Import and Export - Domains are linked by the service objects they share. One domain exports a number of service objects (including their manageability) and these are imported into another domain to create the relationships necessary for that domain.

10.3 MANAGEMENT DIMENSIONS

To understand the relationships between Objects and Functions both within a domain and between domains it is necessary to explore at least three different dimensions of Management.

10.3.1 Management Structure

A domain exists to ensure that a coherent set of objectives and relationships between them provides a desired service to another domain. The structure within a domain reflects 4 levels of management concern within that domain:

i)   SPECIFIC RESOURCE - at this level exists the specific real resources of the domain and any imported service resources from other domain(s). It is out of these resources that a system will be configured to provide services to other domains.

ii)   GENERIC RESOURCE - at this level exists the agreed models that the Specific Resources conform to. This generic conformity allows a system to be built from resources sourced for multiple vendors. Logic exists at this level to map the specific resource onto the model that is required of it. Imported service resources should (if specified properly) already conform to an agreed model and so this level should be transparent.

iii)   SYSTEM - at this level exists the model of the configuration as a whole. The relationships between objects can be seen in the context of whole systems. Logic exists at this level to map system concepts onto identifiable Generic Resources which realize what is required.

iv)   SERVICE RESOURCE - at this level the services supplied by the domain are supported as logical managed objects to allow them to be exported to another domain which imports them as specific resources.

Thus the four level structure within a domain allows issues to be resolved within that domain (if possible) and when they cannot be resolved allows them to be properly escalated to another domain in terms of the service provided. Each domain has one or more service objects that it supports and measurements of attributes associated with those objects provides the basis of a service level agreement between domains.

10.3.2 Management Life Cycle

The management functions within a domain must integrate to support a defined life cycle model for that particular domain. Analysis of where costs are greatest and skills are in short supply shows that only by adopting a Total Life Cycle approach will Management Systems be viable in the 1990's.

By Total Life Cycle it is implied that Planning, Building and Running of Domain specific systems must be supported in a cyclic manner such that information gleaned during Planning is available for Building, information gleaned during Building is available for Running and information gleaned during Running is available for Planning.

The existence and support of this feed forward and feedback loop can be a differentiator for a Systems Management offering in that it can increase automation and decrease the skill levels needed to interpret information at every stage.

10.3.3 Management Areas

The five areas of management chosen by ISO are by no means exhaustive but they give a good indication as to what activities should be undertaken by functional units within a given management domain. The definitions are contained within the OSI Reference Model Management Framework (ISO 7498/4) and in this form they specifically relate to the management of interconnection and interworking Total Systems Management needs to extrapolate those concepts to other aspects of an IT system as well. The OSI NM FORUM in doing this in certain areas for a wider set of objects.

The OSI FIVE are:

CONFIGURATION
FAULT
PERFORMANCE
ACCOUNTING
SECURITY

Work in these areas is tending to refine the definition of managed objects rather than change the management protocols involved.

The analysis of the management functions which support these five areas, and others, and the development of management tools to support them provides good opportunity for differentiation in an Open Systems environment.

10.4 MANAGEMENT DOMAINS

Domains are a concept which is widely used and abused and so it is necessary to be precise about what concepts are imported into Systems Management by the use of the term:

"A Management Domain exists to assure its user that the services it provides will meet the Service Levels agreed upon in advance"

The Management Domain is focused upon the services it assures not simply on the objects it manages; indeed, similar or identical objects may be used in several domains targeted at providing different services. The managed objects within the domain or imported as services from other domains are used to support the supplied services; it is by these supplied (exported) services that the effectiveness of the domain must be measured.

Thus the model of a domain includes:

i) Domain Specific Objects which exist only because they are needed by that domain.

ii) Imported Service Objects which are provided by another domain (or domains).

iii) An Administration which covers all 4 levels of management structure described in section 10.3.l.

iv) Exported Service Objects which meet the needs of one or more domains.

10.5 MANAGEMENT HCI

When considering the HCI aspects of Systems Management the focus is on that small band of users who are responsible for using the Systems Management tools to realize the domains of management chosen. The general users are an important factor in that they are managed objects in their own specific domains and they can help the systems to work by doing specific things.

With respect to Managing users there are three important views to be considered:

i) The Domain Specific view

ii) The Top Level SLA view

iii) The Functional view.

10.5.1 The Domain Specific View

Depending on the nature of the services supplied and the objects being managed in any given domain may have a Managing User Perspective which ranges from User Intensive to almost Automatic. These ranges can be best understood by considering the 3 major parts of the management life cycle.

Planning -   Domain specific planning involves technically skilled resources that understand the managed objects in that domain and the services it supplies. It is not done in real time and may well be aided by expert systems. Systems Integration tends to lead to several domains being planned in a single time frame.

Building -   With adequate tools building should be automated leaving only the need to authorize the various stages of the process to ensure that it fits in with the business as a whole.

Running -   Although the target is to have operator-less running, prior to the realization of that target, there will be the need for users with domain specific knowledge to diagnose problems and re-establish service at the domain level.

The key HCI issue is supporting skilled managing users which have domain specific knowledge.

10.5.2 Top level SLA View

Systems Management is also viewed via the Service Level Agreements that are met (or not, as the case may be); this is a more indirect perspective in that it views the Systems Management by its result <u>not</u> its specific action. In the total solutions market this will be an increasingly important perspective to get right.

10.5.3 Management Functions

The third view is a new one that is potentially created by the Architecture itself but is also valued by the customer community as well. The requirement is currently expressed as "the need for a standard MMI". When one delves more deeply, the requirement is that when a skilled person has learnt how to do a job in one domain they should be able to exercise that skill in other domains. The emphasis on re-use of generic function designs between domains will encourage this to be the case by default.

10.6   SERVICE LEVEL AGREEMENTS

The idea of Service Level Agreements (SLA's) has been touched upon in the context of user views of systems management. The use of Service Level Agreements is becoming a formal discipline for measuring whether an IT system has provided the required service to a set of users both individually and as a corporate whole. The current emphasis on Service Level Agreements is at the IT/User boundary and between organizations which are providing/using each others services.

The key to good Systems Management is to establish SLA's at each Domain boundary whether or not it represents an organizational division of responsibility. Forming and monitoring an SLA for each Domain will identify whether the systems design is cost effective and provide key data for boundary checking when problems exist within the design.

By formalizing the service interface into a functional interface and a set of service objects with attributes it is possible to express SLA's as algorithms based on measured attributes for specific objects. Thus the managed object model not only provides a way of communicating information within and between domains but it also aids the expression of an SLA at each domain interface.

10.7 ENGINEERING FRAMEWORK

The framework discussed above concentrates on aspects of Management Theory and Object Oriented Architecture as a basis for building a Systems Management Architecture. This section introduces the key engineering approaches which will be used to ensure that a total integrated solution to Systems Management is achievable.

10.7.1 3 Part Model

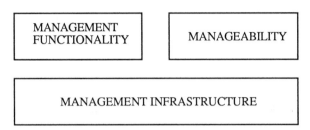

The MANAGEMENT INFRASTRUCTURE provides services for linking the MANAGEABILITY in various products to MANAGEMENT FUNCTIONS. The INFRASTRUCTURE supports de facto and ISO standards for management information exchange and reduces to a minimum the specific implementations of MANAGEABILITY in specific products. The products support well-defined Managed Object models which are shared within the Management Domain(s). Each Management Domain will use MANAGEMENT FUNCTIONALITY as a library generic common components.

10.7.2 Key Interfaces

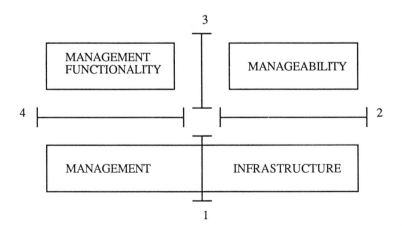

Within the 3 part model for engineering management domains there are 5 key interfaces which are developing and must be formalized to make the structure robust.

1)   The INFORMATION TRANSFER interface covers the protocols and data formats that are used to convey management information between a manager and the agents of the managed objects. The proprietary use of CAM and FTF will role over into use of the CMIP and FTAM profiles (as per OSI NM FORUM).

2)   The ENVIRONMENT interface between the MANAGEMENT INFRASTRUCTURE and MANAGEABILITY within specific products must be moved into the Common Application Environment agenda and developed to a level where as much work as possible is done within the standard infrastructure. The Internal initiatives on this interface currently focus on the Standard Monitoring Interface proposed by Mainframes as part of IDA; this must be rolled out into other key environments.

3)   The CONCEPTUAL interface between MANAGEABILITY and MANAGEMENT FUNCTIONALITY is an agreement on the Managed Object Definitions which will be supported both by the specific products and the Domain Administration into which they fit.

4)   The ENVIRONMENT interface between INFRASTRUCTURE and FUNCTIONALITY is currently a proprietary interface defined to maximize re-use. As we roll out new management functions and wish to make these portable, this too may be the subject of standardization. This is not the case at present with most suppliers regarding Management as an area for differentiation.

5)   The GATEWAY to other proprietary management systems will be supported by the infrastructure on the management side to encourage exploitation of as much of our functionality as possible.

10.7.3 Manageability

The manageability of a given product is achieved by exposing a model of one or more related objects which are viewed as representing the key aspects of the products. Each object has common attributes such as NAME, VERSION, TYPE etc and specific attributes which reflect the nature of the produce concerned. Concepts such as CONTAINMENT, INHERITANCE and RELATIONSHIP allow a rich picture of the product to be modeled and supported, using the ENVIRONMENT interface.

Specific attributes cover issues such as:

STATUS (ADMINISTRATIVE and OPERATIONAL).

PARAMETERS

MEASUREMENTS (several different standard constructs are supported by the Structure of Management Information.

ALERTS (conditions under which events will be generated and notified.

COMMANDS (and RESPONSES).

The environment interface supports all standard attribute types and provides services which help the model to be communicated to relevant Management Functionality.

10.7.4 Generic Functions and Domain Integration

The Administration of a given Domain is built round standard Management Functions which are designed to interact with each other and the standard elements of managed objects in a prescribed manner. The Domain specific flavour of the Administration is added by:

1) Adding 'user' hooks to a standard framework.
2) Encoding specific filter algorithms.
3) Encoding specific aggregation algorithms.
4) Generation of specific reports.
5) Encoding specific escalation rules.
6) Setting specific threshold and trend parameters
    to
    expected values

and so on.

10.8 SUMMARY

This chapter looks at Systems Management from an Architectural viewpoint. It introduces concepts which are emerging as the key features in the managed IT solutions of the 1990's. No matter how good the concepts are, the quality of the solution will always depend on other factors such as Requirement Definition, Engineering, Support, Training, Documentation.

Chapter 11

Data Communications over Cellular Radio

P. J. Munday

11.1   INTRODUCTION

The UK cellular radio networks, Vodafone and Cellnet, started commercial service at the beginning of 1985, following the successful introduction of cellular radio in a number of other countries, predominantly the USA and Scandinavia. The networks offer mobile telephony via 900 MHz radio links and the main features are summarised in Table 11.1.

TABLE 11.1 UK TACS cellular radio system

Service Opened:	1985
Planned UK Coverage: (by 1990)	90% of population 65% of land area
Services Offered:	Mobile telephony - Voice (Predominantly) - Supplementary Services - Data (Small but growing)
Networks:	Vodafone and Cellnet
Frequency Bands:	890 - 905 MHz (Mobile transmit) 935 - 950 MHz (Base transmit)
Modulation:	FM (analogue voice) 8 kb/s FSK (signalling)
Channel spacing:	25 kHz

The radio coverage area is divided into small cells, of radius up to about 16 km, and each cell is served by a radio base station. The base stations are linked by land lines or microwave links to mobile switching centres, MSC's, which are in turn connected to the public switched telephone network (PSTN) as shown in Figure 11.1. The traffic carried is predominantly voice. Use of data communications over the cellular radio networks is a small but growing service.

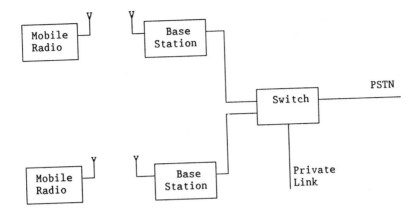

Fig. 11.1 Cellular radio - Outline block diagram

This chapter discusses some of the problems encountered and solutions generated in providing a data communications capability over cellular radio. Both the current UK analogue system (Total Access Communication System-TACS), and the proposed Pan European digital cellular radio system (Groupe Speciale Mobile-GSM), due to start commercial service in 1991, are considered.

11.2   IMPAIRMENTS TO DATA COMMUNICATIONS OVER RADIO LINKS

Data communications over radio links can suffer from much higher levels of transmission errors than over lines. The factors which lead to these errors are as follows (and are illustrated in Figure 11.2):

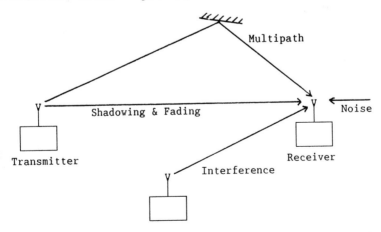

Fig.11.2 Impairments to radio transmission

(a) Noise in the radio receiver circuitry. Received signals can be as low as typically -110 dBm (10-14 watts) and are thus not many dB above circuit noise levels (about - 120 dBm in a typical FM receiver).
(b)   Interference from other radio transmitters, or from other man made sources e.g. car ignition systems.
(c) "Fading" i.e. variations in the level of the received signal.
(d)   "Shadowing" of the transmitter from the receiver by obstacles such as bridges and buildings.   This can result in complete loss of the received signal for periods of time.
(e) "Multipath" effects where the signal arrives at the receiver via several "paths", a direct path and reflections off buildings or hills.

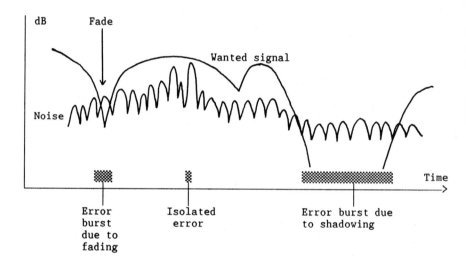

Fig.11.3 Error effects in radio transmission

These factors can lead to both isolated errors and bursts of errors, as illustrated in Figure 11.3.   Typical bit error rates (BER) and error burst (fade) durations are given in Table 11.2 for the TACS cellular radio system. Another cause of errors in data transmission is breaks to allow for the transmission of signalling messages.   One particular example of such a break is when "handover" of a call occurs. (This happens when a mobile moves out of the coverage area of one base station into the coverage area of another, and handover of the call to the new base station is done automatically by the cellular radio network.)   Breaks of up to about 300 ms can occur during handover. Breaks in transmission due to shadowing can be of any length, but after a break of 5 seconds, the cellular radio network will automatically clear down the call.

TABLE 11.2   Error conditions and methods of protection

Error Condition	Typical Values		Method of Protection
Isolated errors due to noise	BER < 2%	)))	Forward Error Correction (FEC) and
Short bursts due to fading	BER < 2% Fades 1-10 ms	))	Interleaving
Signalling breaks (e.g. handover)	100-300 ms	)))	Automatic Repeat
Radio shadows	Up to 5 seconds (before call is cleared down)	)))	Requests (ARQ)

The isolated errors and short bursts of errors can be dealt with by forward error correction (FEC) combined with interleaving. The longer breaks in transmission cannot be dealt with by FEC, and the technique of automatic repeat requests (ARQ) must be used. These are discussed below, with examples of parameters taken from a (public domain) data standard, CDLC (Cellular Data Link Control), used on the Racal Vodafone network.

11.3   FORWARD ERROR CORRECTION

Forward error correction techniques have been known for many years. In essence, a number of "parity bits" are transmitted along with the information bits. The ratio of information bits to information plus parity bits is called the code "redundancy" and in general, the lower the redundancy, the higher the error rates which can be successfully dealt with. Error correcting codes can be divided into 3 main types:

(a)   Binary block codes in which a block of k information bits is coded up with a block of n-k parity bits to give a block of n bits. (This is termed an (n,k) code.)

(b)   Symbol block codes in which the information bits are combined into k symbols (e.g. 5 bit symbols) and n-k parity symbols are added, to give a block of n symbols (an (n,k) code). The most common class of symbol codes are "Reed Solomon" (RS) codes.

(c)   Convolutional codes in which the parity bits are formed by the mathematical process of "convolving" the information bits with a suitable "generator polynomial".
     For block codes, increasing the block length n increases the power of the code, while for convolutional codes increasing the length (constraint length) of the generator polynomial increases the power of the code. However both of these make the code more complex to implement and also increase the delay in transmission.
     The choice of which code to use involves a tradeoff between performance, transmission efficiency (i.e. redundancy) and implementation complexity.

Probability of error
in approx 500 bit message

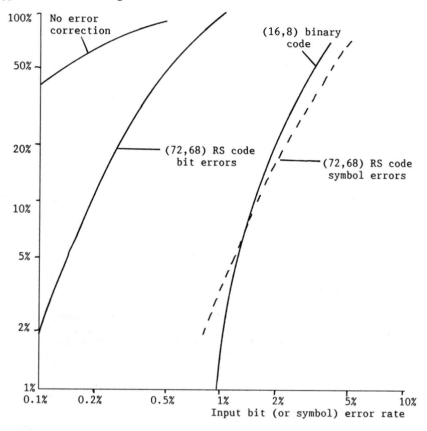

Fig. 11.4 Performance of some error correcting codes

Figure 11.4 shows the performance that can be achieved for several different error correcting codes in terms of the probability that a message will be received error free for a given input bit error rate. In the solid curves in Figure 11.4, it is assumed that the input errors are randomly distributed. However as we saw earlier, the errors often arrive in bursts. Short bursts of errors can be corrected if a process of interleaving is used i.e. instead of transmitting all the bits of one code block together, the bits of a given code block are spread out in time by interleaving bits of other code blocks together, as illustrated in Figure 11.5. The interval between successive bits belonging to the same code block is called the "interleaving depth", and is 10 bit periods in the example in Figure 11.5.

Input blocks:

Block no: A | B | | J

Bit no: 1 2 3 4 5 6 7 8|1 2 3 4 5 6 7 8| . . .|1 2 3 4 5 6 7 8

Transmitted bit stream:

    A1 B1 ... J1 A2 B2 ... J2 .... A8 B8 ... J8

    <──────────>   ▓▓▓▓▓▓▓▓▓▓
    Interleaving   Error
       depth   burst

Blocks at receiver

         A | B | | J

    1 2 3 4 5 6 7 8|1 2 3 4 5 6 7 8| . . .|1 2 3 4 5 6 7 8

        Errors: ▓   ▓

Fig. 11.5   Example of interleaving with block code

Provided the error burst lengths are less than the interleaving depth, the codes can handle burst errors just as well as random errors. Increasing the interleaving depth increases the capability of the code to combat burst errors, but has the disadvantage of increasing the length of the message. The CDLC standard uses a (16,8) binary block code with a range of interleaving depths, as shown in Table 11.3.

TABLE 11.3 Synchronisation and interleaving parameters

Sync Type	Block Length msec	Inter-leaving Depth msec	Information Characters In Block (N)
0	47	1.7	0
1	60	2.5	2
2	73	3.3	4
3	100	5	8
4	153	8.3	16
5	260	15	32
6	473	28.3	64
7	(Use of non-interleaved Reed Solomon (72,68) code)		

An alternative method of dealing with short bursts of errors is by means of Reed Solomon symbol block codes. With a symbol code, it is irrelevant whether a symbol has just one bit in error or many bits in error, there is still a symbol error. For this reason symbol codes are often better at dealing with short bursts of errors than with random errors. Take for example the Reed Solomon (72,68) code (which uses 8 bit symbols) shown in Figure 11.4. This code can correct up to 2 symbols in error. If we have a short error burst of up to 9 bits, at most 2 symbols will be in error, and the code can correct them. If the error burst started at a symbol boundary, error bursts of up to 16 bits could be corrected.

If we interpret the input error rate axis in Figure 11.4 as a symbol error rate, we get a performance as shown by the dotted curve. In practice we find that the performance of the (72,68) Reed Solomon code in the presence of short bursts of errors is slightly to the left of the dotted curve in Figure 11.4, i.e. just slightly below the performance of the (16,8) code with interleaving. However the Reed Solomon Code can allow information rates of 2400 baud to be transmitted, whereas the (16,8) code only allows information rates of just over 1200 baud. The non-interleaved (72,68) code is now an additional code in a new version of the CDLC Standard, this code being selected automatically when the error rate is sufficiently low.

With an FEC and interleaving scheme, it is necessary to synchronise the coding blocks at the receiver. A synchronising sequence can be sent for this purpose, but transmission errors may occur in this sequence. The CDLC standard uses a set of 8 synchronising sequences, each 48 bits long. (The sync sequence used identifies to the receiver the code and interleaving depth used). By contrast, line systems (with very low error rates) use sync sequences only a few bits in length, but no errors in the sync are tolerated.

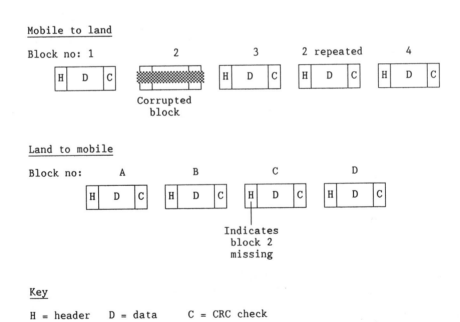

Fig. 11.6 Automatic repeat requests (ARQ)

11.4. AUTOMATIC REPEAT REQUESTS (ARQ)

The principle of Automatic Repeat Requests (ARQ) is illustrated in Figure 11.6. The data to be transmitted is divided into blocks, and to each block is added a header, the whole block then being protected by an error detecting code, normally a "cyclic redundancy check" (CRC). Each block is given a reference number, and the header contains the reference number of the block being transmitted, plus information on the reference number of the last correctly received block. In the example in Figure 11.6, block 2 on the mobile to land link fails to be received correctly. The land terminal then signals the loss of block 2 to the mobile terminal in the header of block C, and the mobile terminal then repeats block 2. ARQ techniques enable long bursts of errors, which may affect several blocks, to be corrected. The main drawback of ARQ is a variable delay in the transmission of data, which has to be allowed for either by having large buffer stores at the terminals, or by using "flow control" where the data terminal is commanded to stop transmitting data while blocks are being repeated. ARQ can be combined with FEC to give a powerful error correction capability, able to deal with virtually all types of errors encountered on radio links.

The ARQ system in CDLC is based on the procedures of the "HDLC" standard, with the use of selective reject.

11.5. ADDITION OF DATA SERVICES TO CELLULAR RADIO

The UK cellular radio networks are predominantly voice networks, with data services a small but growing requirement. A subscriber who wishes to use data on cellular radio can of course add suitable equipment to his mobile radio terminal. However the other end of the radio link, one of several hundred base stations, is not under his control, and for the cellular operators, it would have been uneconomic to add expensive data communications equipment at each base station to service the initially very small number of data users. It was therefore decided on the Racal Vodafone network to use "voice band" modems between the data terminals and the radio network, so that the radio network could handle data "transparently", as if it were voice traffic.

TABLE 11.4 2 Wire full duplex modem standards

Modem Type	Bit Rate	Modulation	Equalisation	Scrambler
V21	300/300	FSK	No	No
V23	1200/75	FSK	No	No
V26 bis	2400/150	QPSK/FSK	Fixed	Optional
V22	1200/1200	QPSK	Fixed	Yes
V22 bis	2400/2400	16 point APK	Adaptive	Yes
V27 ter	4800/75	8 phase PSK/FSK	Adaptive	Yes

There is benefit in having a single standard for the radio link in that a single piece of equipment in the mobile station can be used to access various data services by the provision of interworking functions to these services within the network. A number of possible modem standards were considered and these are listed in Table 11.4. "2 wire" full duplex modems only were considered because most users require some form of duplex operation, and ARQ schemes are more efficient and have lower delay if a full duplex link is available. (See below for a discussion on "2 wire" systems). A number of problems with some of these modems were identified:

(a) The cellular radio equipment uses a process of   syllabic "companding" for voice to improve the voice quality in the presence of fading. This companding distorts the amplitude modulation of the V22 bis modem.

(b) Fading on the radio link can impair the operation of the adaptive equalisers in the V22 bis and V27 ter modems.

(c)   The   "polynomial" scramblers which are used in the V22 bis   and V27 ter modems lead to "error multiplication", i.e. the error rates are increased by 2-3 times, as illustrated in Figure 11.7. This is not a problem for lines, where error rates are very low, but is a problem for radio links where the typically 2% error rates would become   4-6%   and would require more powerful error correction techniques.

For these reasons, the V26 bis modem was selected for CDLC. In order to test its performance over real radio links, some experimental trials were undertaken, both with and without forward error correction.

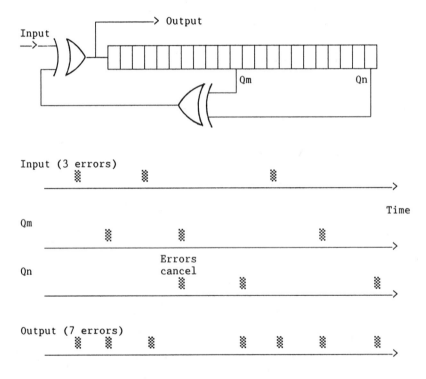

Fig. 11.7 Error multiplication in a polynomial scrambler

The results were sorted according to received signal strength and vehicle speed, and are summarised in Table 11.5. It can be seen that the results get worse for lower received signal strengths (as might be expected) and also in general get worse for higher vehicle speeds (due to the higher rate of fading). With FEC however, virtually all the errors get corrected and the small percentage of block failures due to uncorrected errors can easily be dealt with by ARQ. The limit signal strength for voice communications is about -110 dBm, at which level the error corrected data scheme works very well. Thus at least as good a cellular coverage area is achievable for data as for voice.

TABLE 11.5 Summary of field trials results

Physical Conditions		Percentage Block errors (after FEC)			
		2400 baud Channel 512 data bits		150 baud Channel 36 data bits	
Speed km/hr	Signal Strength dBm	No FEC	Interleaved 16, 8 code	No FEC	Interleaved 23, 12 code
0.20	-120 to -110	23.7	0.6	8.8	0.0
0-20	-110 to -100	17.5	0.6	5.3	0.0
0-20	-100 to -90	11.1	1.0	5.4	0.0
0-20	-90 to -80	8.3	0.0	4.5	0.0
20-40	-120 to -110	49.8	0.0	24.2	0.0
20-40	-110 to -100	42.6	0.0	23.1	0.0
20-40	-100 to -90	27.8	0.2	11.7	0.0
20-40	-90 to -80	18.1	0.0	4.4	0.0
40-75	-120 to -110	58.5	1.7	---	---
40-75	-110 to -100	36.1	0.0	---	---
40-75	-100 to -90	29.2	0.6	4.2	4.2
40-75	-90 to -80	17.8	0.0	2.0	2.0

Figure 11.8 illustrates in outline form how the data services are supported on the cellular network. The cellular modems (which contain a voice band modem and FEC and ARQ functions) are located at the mobile radios, and at various locations in the land network, as follows:

(a) For a call via the PSTN, between the PSTN and the data terminal.
(b) For a call via a private network, between the private network and the data terminal.
(c) For a call via a packet switch network (e.g. PSS), at the MSC between the switch and the "Packet Assembler/Disassembler" (PAD).
(d) For a call via a modem pool, between the switch and the modem pool.

It should be noted that the PSTN is a "2 wire" network where the transmitted and received signals are passed down the same pair of wires, while all the other links in Figure 11.8 are "4 wire", i.e. the transmitted and received signals are passed down separate pairs of wires. With the use of the V26 bis modem, two separate cases can be considered:

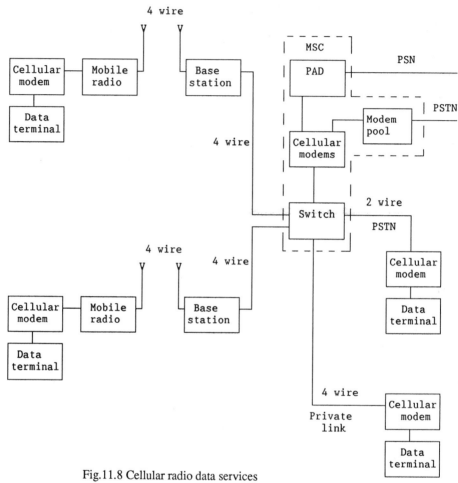

Fig.11.8 Cellular radio data services

(i) When the call involves a direct PSTN path, the V26 bis modem is automatically operated in 2 wire mode, 2400 baud in one direction and 150 baud in the opposite direction. A protocol in the cellular modems at each end of the link enables a decision to be made about which end transmits at 2400 baud. The decision is based on which end has the most data to send, and the protocol enables the decision to be reversed as necessary during the call if it is found that the other end of the link has a lot of data to send.

(ii) Calls from a mobile to a private network, packet switched network, modem pool, or to another mobile all have 4 wire paths available throughout, in which case 4 wire operation of the modems is used, each end of the link both transmitting and receiving at 2400 baud.

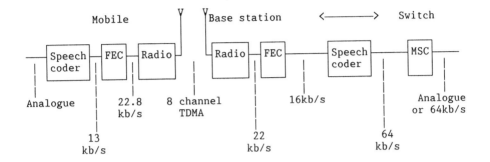

Fig.11.9 Speech on Pan European (GSM) cellular radio system

11.6. THE PAN EUROPEAN CELLULAR RADIO SYSTEM (GSM)

The Pan European (Groupe Speciale Mobile - GSM) cellular radio system is planned for commercial service in 1991. Unlike the TACS analogue system, the GSM system employs a digital speech coder, and the all digital nature of the transmissions enhances the possibilities for data transmission. Figure 11.9 shows in outline the way voice transmission is handled in the GSM system. The voice is digitised at 13 kb/s, and FEC is then applied to give a data rate of 22.8 kb/s. Up to 8 simultaneous voice transmissions are then multiplexed onto a single radio frequency carrier by a process of time division multiple access (TDMA). On the land side, the speech coder can be placed at the base station, in which case the base station to switch link uses 64 kb/s PCM coding (a standard for digital telephony). Alternatively the speech coder can be placed at the switch in which case the base station to switch link operates at 16 kb/s (13 kb/s for speech plus some control information), and 4 simultaneous voice transmissions can then be multiplexed onto a single 64 kb/s channel.

The system allows for the future evolution of "half rate" speech coders which, after FEC, give a data rate of 11.4 kb/s. This would allow up to 16 simultaneous voice transmissions per radio frequency carrier.

As for the TACS system, data transmission will be a small but growing service on the GSM system, and the same economic considerations about the addition of data services apply. The FEC used for voice and signalling on GSM is a flexible scheme using convolutional codes, with interleaving over 4 or 8 TDMA frames (of length approximately 5 ms). For virtually no additional complexity, the same FEC scheme can be adapted for data services at various rates. In fact a concession was made for data services by allowing interleaving over 19 TDMA frames to improve performance for the higher data rates. This has only a small cost impact provided it is allowed for at the start of the design of the system.

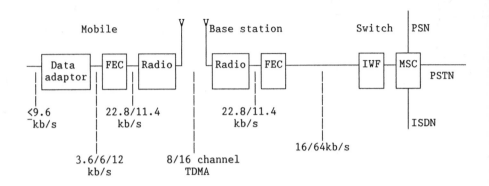

Fig.11.10 Data services implementation on GSM system

Figure 11.10 illustrates how data services are handled over the GSM system. A data adaptor at the mobile converts the data (at rates up to 9.6 kb/s) into a standard "ISDN like" format at rates of either 3.6, 6 or 12 kb/s. (The format is in fact ISDN but with certain synchronisation and other bits removed. These bits are unnecessary in view of the synchronisation process already in use in the GSM system). FEC is then applied to give a data rate of either 22.8 kb/s (full rate), or 11.4 kb/s (half rate). On the land side, FEC is performed at the base station (unlike in the CDLC standard on TACS where it is performed at the switch or at the land subscriber's location). An interworking function (IWF) at the switch then converts the data into the formats required for interworking with the PSTN, a packet switched network or ISDN.

Two types of service are available, "transparent" which uses just FEC, and "non transparent" which uses both FEC and an ARQ scheme known as RLP(Radio Link Protocol) in order to obtain a good quality of service.

TABLE 11.6 Data services available on GSM system

Data Rate	Channel	Convolutional Code Redundancy	Interleaving Block Length
9.6 kb/s	Full rate	61/114 = 0.53	95 ms
4.8 kb/s	Full rate	1/3	95 ms
4.8 kb/s	Half rate	61/114	190 ms
<2.4 kb/s	Full rate	1/6	40 ms
<2.4 kb/s	Half rate	1/3	190 ms
(Speech	Full rate	Variable 1/2 or 1	40 ms)
(Signalling	-	1/2	20/40 ms)

Table 11.6 shows the range of data services that will be supported on the GSM system, and shows how the FEC and interleaving for data is at least as good, if not better, than for voice and signalling, thus ensuring that the cellular coverage area for data will be at least as good as for voice.

The GSM system will thus be able to provide reliable data transmission at user rates up to 9.6 kb/s.

Chapter 12

Broadcast Systems with Data Capability

J. P. Chambers

12.1 INTRODUCTION

Broadcast services began with sound radio in the 1920s, followed by television in the 1930s. Since the early 1970s there has been increasing interest in the use of data broadcasting, in the words of the BBC's Royal Charter, 'as a means of disseminating information, education and entertainment'.

Some data broadcasting services are intended to display information on suitably-equipped television or radio receivers. The teletext system allows pages of text to appear on the television screen, with the possibility of subtitles and newsflashes inserted in the normal picture. One feature of RDS allows short messages to appear on an alphanumeric display on a radio receiver.

Other data broadcasting services are intended to provide information for devices peripheral to a domestic broadcast receiver, such as the telesoftware service for home computers. Yet others provide a more restricted service for particular applications, such as Datacast and Radio Teleswitching.

Until recently, sound and vision broadcasting has always used analogue techniques and data capacity has been added as an extra facility. Digital sound is now available in domestic equipment (the Compact Disc) and some television receivers now convert the vision signal into digital form for processing. Systems for broadcasting sound in digital form are now in use, and digital methods of broadcasting vision signals are under study. Some systems, such as the MAC/packet multiplex and NICAM 728 are so new that the uses of their spare data capacity have not yet emerged.

This chapter describes the technical basis of the main broadcasting systems capable of carrying data in current and potential use in the UK. Many of the principles used in other data communications networks will be found in these examples, together with some features peculiar to broadcasting. Some mention is made of different systems in use in other countries. The EBU-approved MAC/packet family of systems for satellite broadcasting is described, but no attempt is made to survey other possible satellite data broadcasting systems.

The systems to be discussed in detail are summarized in Table 12.1.

12.2 ASPECTS OF BROADCAST SYSTEMS

There are many differences between a broadcast network and a typical data communications network. Existing sound and television networks provide almost complete coverage nationwide with high reliability. So when a data system is added to an existing network it enjoys the benefit of an immediate wide range of potential users. There are thousands of transmitters but tens of millions of receivers. The market size is such that mass production techniques are used in receiver manufacture and components, notably integrated circuits and display tubes, are developed

TABLE 12.1 SUMMARY OF BROADCASTING SYSTEMS CAPABLE OF CARRYING DATA

SYSTEM	CARRIER	TYPE	MODULATION	PEAK bit/s	MEAN bit/s	BLOCK LENGTH	USEFUL LENGTH	CRC	Additional details
on-screen TV signalling	patches on picture		NRZ brightness	25	25				photo-electric pick-up attached to TV screen
radio telesoftware	sound channel		FSK	1200	1200	8k*		16	higher bit rates possible using VHF/FM audio channels
LFradio-data	LF radio		bi-phase + PM	25	25	50	32	13	used on 198kHz for 'teleswitching' service
RDS	VHF/FM radio	FDM	bi-phase + DSBSCAM	1187.5	1187.5	26	16	10	data differentially encoded to avoid carrier ambiguity
SCA	VHF/FM radio	FDM	FSK*	4800*					transmissions using various standards
teletext (1)	television	TDM	NRZ	6.9375M	(2) 144k	360	320		CRC on block groups (pages)
Datacast	"	"	"	"	(3) 54k	360	288	16	variable address length
NICAM 728	television	FDM	DQPSK	728 k	11k	728	11		scrambled, bit-interleaved
-mono sound					363k	728	715+		"
- no sound					715k	728	715		"
C-MAC/packet	television	TDM	2-4 PSK	20.25 M	(4) 3.0M	751	728		scrambled, bit-interleaved
D-MAC/packet	"	"	duobinary	20.25 M	(4) 3.0M	751	728		"
D2-MAC/packet	"	"	duobinary	10.125M	(4) 1.5M	751	728		"

(1) including teletext telesoftware, and page-organised data broadcasting
(2) assuming eight lines per television field
(3) assuming three lines per television field
(4) this includes as many (digital) sound signals as are required at that time

* typical
+ alternating with 11

primarily for this market. The economies of scale have reduced the real cost of receivers steadily over the years and these benefits apply also to receivers for associated data services. Because of the one-to-many nature of broadcasting it is worthwhile to concentrate difficult or expensive operations at the source rather than to divide them between source and receiver.

In most parts of the country it is very easy to receive broadcast services, no wires need to be laid and there is no waiting time.

12.2.1 Problems of Broadcast Systems

New broadcast systems, particularly additions to existing systems, have to be developed with great care. It is most important that they do not interfere with the normal operation of receivers already purchased and in use, even if they are over ten years old. The designer of a new system does not know how many different types of receiver are in use, and how well they are aligned and maintained. In the limit, the only way to prove the compatibility of a new system is by carefully controlled tests using the public network.

Users of a new service expect to be able to receive it without problem if they already enjoy good reception of the associated sound or television service. This too constrains the designer of a new system. The successful introduction of stereo radio and colour television required careful planning over many years.

International agreements cover the allocation of transmitter frequencies and powers, and there are agreed tolerances which allow new services to be planned without interfering with existing services. Whereas telecommunications authorities can provide gateways with agreed interfaces between countries, there are no rigid boundaries to broadcasting. The cross-border and satellite reception of broadcast services makes the work of the European Broadcasting Union (EBU) and International Radio Consultative Committee (CCIR) towards common standards increasingly important.

In most cases, data systems have been added on to existing services where there has been little spare signalling capacity within the channel. In order to make best use of this unique and very limited resource, the overheads such as synchronization and error control need to be kept very low and special techniques have been developed. The pattern of errors can vary very widely between different users at the same time and there is, of course, no return path available for use in error correction.

The very accessibility of broadcast signals without the need to make a physical connection makes it particularly difficult to ensure the privacy of any messages intended only for a limited audience, such as would be required in a subscription service. Considerable work has been done on developing such one-way access control methods for television and the key management techniques can be applied directly to data broadcasting [1].

Unlike the data service provider, the broadcaster has no control over the manufacture of receivers or the preference of the consumer. This makes it essential that the technical specification of any new service be complete and unambiguous so that it can be interpreted consistently anywhere in the world. Even then there may be problems, and difficult decisions may need to be taken with several thousand sets already sold and in use. Such problems are very much more likely in digital systems as it becomes impossible to check the response to all possible bit pattern combinations and as receiver designers take a pride in providing their own special features by augmenting the decoder software.

12.3 METHODS OF ADDING DATA CAPABILITY

All the systems listed in Table 12.1 have been additions to existing broadcast systems, with the exception of the MAC/packet family of systems [2] which was conceived as a new television standard incorporating a packet multiplex primarily to carry digital sound but with spare data capacity.

12.3.1 Substitution

Perhaps the simplest method of providing data capacity in a sound or television channel is to use all or part of that channel itself to carry data. The use of a broadcast sound channel to carry data was pioneered in the Netherlands in 1978 in a technical magazine called 'Hobbyscoop'. Software for various home computers was broadcast ('radio telesoftware') as a sound signal of the form commonly used to record data and programs on a domestic audio cassette recorder. A highest common factor language 'BASICODE' was devised and software published for interpreting this on several popular home computers.

As well as being used on the VHF/FM network these transmissions were broadcast using the MF and HF transmissions and enjoyed by enthusiasts overseas. In 1984 the BBC broadcast software using this same standard as part of a radio programme called 'Chip Shop'. These radio telesoftware transmissions required no special equipment to receive them, only a radio cassette recorder, or a cable linking the audio output of a radio to a cassette recorder,were needed.

Channel 4 television in the UK carried a programme '4 Computer Buffs' in which data was transmitted by a pulsating patch on the picture using a conventional asynchronous serial data protocol with two brightness levels corresponding to binary zero and one. A photoreceptor was held on the screen by a sucker or an adhesive pad and a small interface board provided a standard logic signal for coupling to a computer.

Clearly both of these substitution techniques intrude into the normal use of the broadcast channel. Although a flashing patch in the corner of the screen is not likely to inconvenience a viewer who happened to find that service the high-level mid-band audio signals of radio telesoftware come as a shock to an unprepared listener. They are unlikely to find regular use in normal programmes although they are well suited to the applications in which they have been used.

The superior audio bandwidth and signal-to-noise ratio of a VHF/FM sound broadcasting channel can support data rates of 4800 bit/s and above.

12.3.2 Mixed Modulation

The LF radio-data service [3] uses phase modulation applied to the carrier of an amplitude-modulated radio transmitter. In order to minimize interference with the normal operation of existing receivers the peak-to-peak phase deviation is restricted to 45° and the bit rate corresponds to frequencies below the audio passband. Because the 198kHz carrier signal is widely used as a frequency standard, the data to be broadcast is first biphase coded so that every data bit provides a complementary pair of phase changes and there is never any aggregate phase change. Moreover, the data clock is normally obtained by direct division of the carrier frequency so that the modulation is coherent.

12.3.3 Frequency-division multiplex (FDM)

Data to be added to a signal using the FDM technique is first modulated on a subcarrier. Two of the systems listed in Table 12.1 insert this data modulation into the signal which in turn modulates a VHF/FM radio transmitter. A third adds the data modulation to a video signal which is then transmitted using vestigial sideband amplitude modulation.

12.3.3.1 FDM on FM sound systems   Figure 12.1a shows the spectrum of the signal modulating a VHF/FM transmitter. Originally these signals carried only a monophonic sound signal with a bandwidth of 15kHz. Later the pilot-tone stereo system, which had been designed for compatibility with existing receivers, was introduced. The left-minus-right stereo difference signal is amplitude modulated using double sideband suppressed carrier on a 38kHz subcarrier. The stereo difference signal, like any other sound signal, is bipolar with a symmetric long-term amplitude

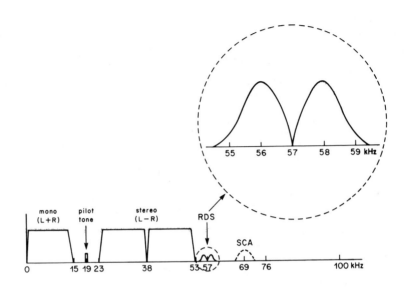

(a) baseband spectrum of VHF/FM sound signal

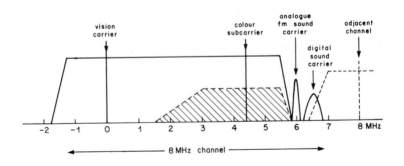

(b) i.f. spectrum of system I television signal

Fig.12.1 - Data broadcasting using FDM techniques.

distribution function centred on silence. The use of suppressed carrier modulation means that there is no energy present in this part of the spectrum when there is no signal, and this minimizes any interference effects. In order to demodulate this signal a 19kHz pilot tone, obtained by frequency division of the 38kHz carrier, is added to the signal. This, of course, conveniently appears midway between the monophonic signal and the lower sideband of the difference signal. This frequency is doubled in the decoder to drive the demodulator.

Clearly there must be a limit to this extension of the spectrum of the modulating signal, and CCIR Recommendation 450-1 provides for a maximum carrier frequency of 76kHz. In practice it is not a sudden limit and it depends on the assumptions made in planning the transmitter network, in particular the spacing of the VHF channels. In Europe this spacing is 100kHz and in North America it is 200kHz. So there is potential for including other services at the upper end of the modulating spectrum. But as the transmitter carrier power and peak frequency deviation are also fixed by planning agreement every extra signal will degrade the reception of the existing sound service to a slight extent. An extra signal could also produce unwanted effects in existing stereo or monophonic radio receivers, due perhaps to intermodulation effects. So any new system must be tested rigorously for compatibility.

The VHF/FM radio data system, RDS [4] was developed from work done by the Swedish Telecommunications Administration on a paging system. It is based on the use of a carrier at 57kHz, which is phase-locked to the third harmonic of the pilot tone when present. This means that many of the possible sources of interference become constant or even zero frequency so reducing their subjective annoyance. Advantage in decoder design is gained by locking the data clock to the subcarrier and the rate of 1187.5 bits/s follows from the division of 57kHz by 48.

A system developed in Federal Germany to alert road users to broadcast traffic announcements, known as Autofahrer Rundfunk Information (ARI), also uses information on a 57kHz subcarrier and the RDS system was required to be compatible with ARI. The messages in ARI are carried as single tones of low frequency (125Hz and below) amplitude modulated on the 57kHz carrier, so the data modulation used for RDS provides a null at 57kHz with very little energy to interfere with the sideband of ARI tones. Conversely the ARI sidebands occupy a small portion of the RDS spectrum as shown in the inset to Figure 12.1a.

Within the USA a system known as 'storecasting', because of its use to provide background music in shops, but more formally known there as Subsidiary Communications Authorization (SCA), has been in use for many years. It uses a subcarrier at about 69kHz which is frequency modulated by the sound signal. Some services carry more than one SCA signal on separate subcarriers, and the ARI service is also in use on some transmitters. In some cases SCA carries data services and frequency-shift keying is then used. In the UK at the time of writing (early 1989) two Independent Local Radio stations in London are carrying data services of this type, with a data rate of 4800 bits/s.

In the USA the Broadcast Television Systems Committee (BTSC) has defined a multichannel television sound (MTS) system which is frequency modulated on a carrier accompanying the vision signal. It uses the pilot-tone stereo system for the main television sound signal, but with the pilot tone corresponding to their television line frequency (H) of 15734Hz to minimize interference problems between sound and vision. The stereo difference signal is centred on 2H and a Separate Audio Program (SAP) signal is frequency modulated on a 5H subcarrier. It has been proposed that this SAP channel, intended for a second language, carry alternatively data at 19.2kbits/s using FSK or BPSK. A further narrow-band FM signal (NPC) on a carrier at 6.5H is also specified. This too could carry data services.

12.3.3.2 FDM in television systems   The UHF UK television signal (System I) is shown in Figure 12.1b. The vision signal has a nominal bandwidth of 5.5MHz and it is amplitude modulated on the vision carrier with a vestigial lower sideband. Within the vision signal, which is predominantly the brightness (luminance) component, two colour difference signals are carried using suppressed carrier QAM with a subcarrier at about 4.43MHz. The monophonic analogue sound signal is frequency modulated on a carrier 6MHz above the vision carrier. The service is planned with a 8MHz channel spacing so there is little free spectrum (see Figure 12.1b) between the sound carrier and the vestigial lower sideband of an interfering signal on the next higher channel. In continental Europe systems with nominal vision bandwidth 5MHz, 5.5MHz sound subcarrier and channel spacing of 7MHz (System B) or 8MHz (System G) are in use. An extra FM sound carrier is sometimes used to provide a second language sound service, or the two can be combined together to provide a pair of sound channels for stereophony.

In the UK a system for carrying a 728kbit/s data multiplex on a carrier at 6.552MHz has been adopted, primarily for carrying two digital sound channels for stereophony or second language applications [5]. Differentially encoded quadrature phase-shift keying (DQPSK) is used and the bandwidth of the resulting signal is about 728kHz, as indicated in Figure 12.1b. Tests have shown that it can be added compatibly to the UK television network. In countries using Systems B and G the same multiplex rate can be carried on a 5.85MHz carrier with the DQPSK signal filtered to about 510kHz bandwidth.

This system is known as NICAM 728, from Near-Instantaneous Companded Audio Multiplex and the bit rate. The NIC technique involves quantizing the sound signal to 14-bit accuracy and then reducing the accuracy of each 1ms block of samples to at most 10 bits per sample according to one of seven coding ranges. The sample rate is 32kHz, one parity bit is added per sample, and the coding range is signalled by modifying the parity bits [6], so each sound channel requires 352kbit/s. Synchronization and control require 13kbit/s and 11kbit/s capacity is available for use to carry additional data. In the event that either sound channel is not in use its 352kbit/s capacity becomes available as a data service, with neither in use the total useful data capacity is 715kbit/s. More than one European country has expressed interest in using the NICAM 728 system to carry data services.

12.3.4 Time-division multiplex (TDM)

The vision waveform has always contained a significant proportion (25% in system I) of time not devoted to the active picture information. A sound signal has no edges, so there is no need to signal where they are. A vision signal is scanned left to right (lines) and top to bottom (fields) and it is necessary to indicate the boundaries of the lines and fields within the waveform itself. In order to keep the receiver scanning circuits simple, relatively long periods of non-picture (known as blanking) are provided to allow the scanning waveform to be reset and to restart its linear progression. For some of this time early in the blanking periods the waveform is taken to a synchronization level outside the white-to-black amplitude range, which triggers the scanning processes in the receiver.

The time allowed for line flyback is 12μs in 64μs, and that for field flyback is 1.6ms in 20ms. These, together with the synchronizing pulses and burst of colour subcarrier frequency to lock the colour demodulator, are shown in Figure 12.2a drawn as if the waveform were itself scanned as a picture. Conventional 625-line television scanning uses interlaced fields where each field scan corresponds to only 312.5 lines. This means that two successive fields produce interleaved scan lines to provide the complete picture.

The 625-line television waveform was designed over 25 years ago and even the oldest receivers still in use have a better field scan flyback time than was originally assumed. So it has become possible to include new information in part of the vertical blanking interval (VBI), the 25 unused lines between active fields. Broadcasters have taken advantage of the VBI for many years to insert test signals to allow the distribution and transmission network to be monitored, and various signals have been added for control and switching purposes. Provided such signals appear like valid vision waveforms, and that they do not come too early in the VBI (where they would interfere with synchronization), the worst that can happen is that they appear   at very

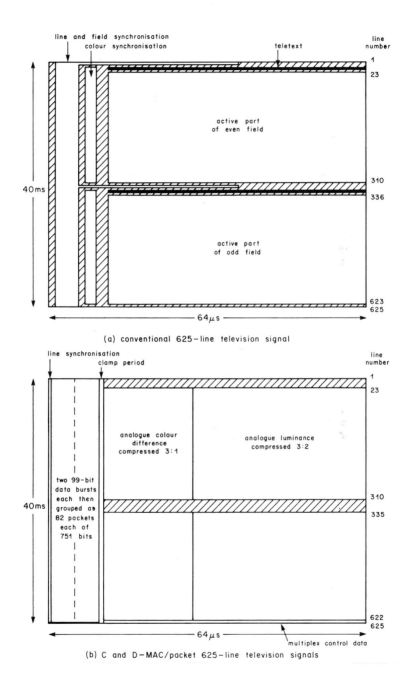

(a) conventional 625-line television signal

(b) C and D-MAC/packet 625-line television signals

Fig.12.2 - 625 - Data broadcasting using TDM techniques..

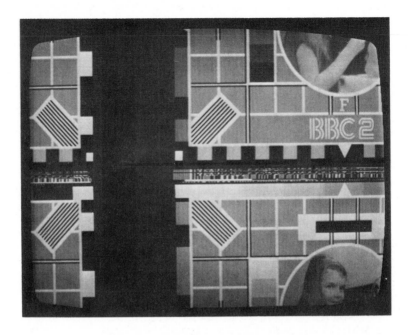

Fig.12.3.(a) - A conventional television display with scans offset to show teletext data in the field-blanking interval.

Fig.12.3.(b) - A MAC/packet waveform displayed on a conventional television screen to show data bursts, and compressed chrominance and luminance.

top of the displayed picture on a domestic receiver. Many receivers include circuitry to suppress such VBI signals so they cannot appear on the screen even if within the area of the display scans. The teletext system [7] was developed in the early 1970s when it was foreseen that it would soon be practicable to equip domestic television receivers with data acquisition, storage and display circuitry using Large Scale Integration (LSI) for a small additional cost. The original motive was to carry subtitles but it was soon realized that it could provide a full new service, complementary to television and radio. In addition to subtitling and the normal service of pages (such as Ceefax and Oracle) other services not intended for direct display on a domestic receiver can be carried as teletext pages. The BBC provides a telesoftware service whereby software for domestic and educational use is distributed on specially coded teletext pages and commercial television offers subscription data services organized as teletext pages.

Figures 12.2a and 12.3a indicate the position of teletext data lines in the television waveform. When teletext services began in 1974 two lines per field were used. Now about eight lines per field are used and the number can be increased to a maximum of 16 when compatibility with existing receivers allows, and providing the other uses of the VBI, such as test signals, can be accommodated in someway.

When the teletext specification was written certain codes were deliberately reserved to allow the transport mechanism of teletext to be used to carry other services which would not interfere with normal teletext reception. Datacast [8] is such a service.

12.3.5 Dedicated multiplex

Work in the EBU towards a new common European standard for 625-line satellite television led to the MAC/packet family of systems [2]. For reasons of compatibility the PAL and SECAM colour systems carry the colour information within the luminance passband. Although spectral overlap is minimized disturbing interaction between the two ('cross-colour') can arise in the decoder, as it is impossible to separate the two components in a normal picture.

A new system is not bound by compatibility and the colour and luminance components are carried in sequence by time division multiplex in the MAC (Multiplexed Analogue Component) system. Because different bandwidths are required these components are compressed (that is, the waveforms are 'speeded up') by a factor 3:2 for luminance and 3:1 for colour. Both line and field blanking intervals are still provided, but they are all available for use. Indeed, the whole layout of the multiplex can be varied by data carried in line 625. The basic format for 625/50 television with standard 4:3 aspect ratio is shown in Figure 12.2b. Apart from transitions and a reference clamp level the remainder of the line period carries a packet data multiplex. For reasons of compatibility with the D2-MAC system of reduced capacity the C- and D-MAC system data multiplex is split in two equal parts. Each carries 99 bits per line and corresponding contributions from successive lines are joined to form a data stream which is then divided into fixed length (751-bit) packets starting from a fixed reference point. A photograph of the MAC/packet waveform displayed on a conventional television receiver is shown in Figure 12.3b.

The prime purpose of the MAC/packet data multiplex is to carry the sound services required for the programme. As many as eight high quality monophonic sound signals can be carried within the capacity of the C- and D-MAC systems, and lower quality sound options are available, for example for sports commentary in many languages. To the extent that the multiplex is not fully populated by sound packets, which of course must be given priority since sound cannot wait, there is capacity available for any type of data service including, for example, a teletext service. It is expected that decoders for the MAC/packet family of systems will provide access to the serial data streams of the packet multiplex for other uses.

12.4   DATA MODULATION

A wide variety of the common methods of data modulation are to be found in data broadcasting systems, and the background to the selection of some of these techniques is now given.

12.4.1 Non Return-to-Zero (NRZ)

This very simple technique is used in on-screen signalling where a minimal-cost receiver and decoder are needed. As an asynchronous protocol with start and stop bits is used there is no problem over clock recovery.

It is also used in teletext [7] and Datacast where a rugged system with high bit rate is required within the vision bandwidth of 5.5MHz (5MHz in continental Europe). The use of odd parity bytes in teletext ensures at most 14 bit periods between data transitions, so simple clock regenerators can be used. More recent decoders use phaselock techniques based on the clock run-in sequence and they can maintain correct clock phase regardless of data transitions in the line. This possibility was anticipated in the teletext specification where the clock tolerance was set at one centicycle per line (25 parts per million). The Datacast specification allows the possibility of totally transparent operation with no restriction on long strings of zeros or ones.

The instantaneous bit rate of teletext is 6.9375 Mbit/s, 444 times line frequency. The recommended pulse spectrum [9] is a 70% raised-cosine roll-off, which is skew symmetric about half the bit rate and reaches zero within the passband. Logic zero corresponds to television black level, logic one to 66% of white level. This reduced level minimizes interference on poorly aligned television sound demodulators yet still allows good decoding of teletext even when the noise is such that picture quality is unacceptable.

12.4.2 Biphase

LF radio-data uses biphase data to phase modulate the carrier in order to provide equal and opposite disturbances to the carrier phase for every data bit. Because there is no long-term accumulation of phase change the carrier remains useful as a standard frequency source.

This absence of a zero frequency component in the biphase signal also explains its use in the RDS system where it is required to minimize energy around the 57kHz carrier to provide compatibility with ARI.

12.4.3 Frequency Shift Keying (FSK)

Radio telesoftware uses FSK as it is the standard in common use for the domestic interchange of computer data and software using audio cassette recorders. The system using a single cycle of 1200Hz or two cycles of 2400Hz to provide binary signalling at 1200 bit/s is low cost, well established and adequately rugged for this purpose.

The use of FSK to carry data on an SCA channel is consistent with the idea of treating the channel as if it were a one-way telephone line over which a modem is used.

12.4.4 Phase Shift Keying (PSK)

LF radio-data uses low deviation PSK to convey additional information on a carrier without interfering with the normal amplitude modulated sound service. In order to ensure precise and stable spectrum shaping the biphase waveform for the linear phase modulator is generated by direct digital waveform synthesis.

The suppressed-carrier amplitude modulation of 57kHz by the biphase RDS data is equivalent to a form of two-phase PSK with a deviation of +90 .

NICAM 728 uses differentially encoded quadrature phase shift keying (QPSK), also known as four-phase differentially encoded phase shift keying (DPSK). This is four-state phase modulation in which each change of state conveys two data bits. The choice of system is dictated mainly by the need to achieve optimum performance within a very tightly controlled bandwidth, although vestigial sideband binary PSK (VSB2-PSK) [10], which had been considered by the EBU for use as a digital modulation system for satellite systems using a subcarrier, was also thought to be suitable.

The C-MAC/packet system switches between two modulation systems at television line rate. The analogue vision components are carried by frequency modulation and the digital information is carried using 2-4 PSK. A one is signalled by a +90° phase change and zero by a -90° change. This is very similar to FSK and it is possible to use the same frequency discriminator for the analogue components and for the data. However, the 2-4 PSK system was chosen to give the best possible error performance when using the entire satellite channel under adverse carrier-to-noise ratios and a more complex demodulator, using differential or coherent techniques, is necessary for best results.

12.4.5 Duobinary

In the D- and D2-MAC/packet systems the binary data stream is converted into a three-level signal using the duobinary technique, and the resulting signal is frequency modulated along with the MAC signal. Conversion to duobinary form concentrates the spectral energy into the region below half the binary signalling rate. So the data component of the D- system has a spectral content comparable to that of the compressed vision signal and that of the D2- system, where the data rate is halved, is suitable for distribution by cable systems using vestigial sideband amplitude modulation.

12.4.6 Differential encoding

The principle of differential encoding where, for example, an incoming logic 1 causes a change of output state whereas a logic 0 leaves the output state unchanged, can be used to eliminate any ambiguity in the polarity of a binary signalling system. It does, however, cause error extension in that a single bit error in the channel causes errors in two consecutive decoded bits.

Differential encoding is used in RDS to avoid ambiguity in the phase of the 57kHz signal required to demodulate the data. In a two-bit, four-level form it is used in NICAM 728 to avoid the need for an absolute reference carrier phase to demodulate the signal. It is used prior to duobinary coding in the D- and D2-MAC/packet systems in such a way that a continuous logic 0 input results in a continuous mid-level output whereas a continuous logic 1 input gives a continuous high or a continuous low output.

12.4.7 Bit-interleaving

Because there is correlation between successive samples of a digital sound signal it is possible effectively to mask the effect of known isolated errors by interpolation between adjoining sound samples. So the NICAM 728 and MAC/packet systems, whose data broadcasting function is primarily to distribute sound in digital form, re-order the bits before transmission and, in a complementary way, after reception in order that bursts of errors in the channel will be converted to isolated errors in the final data stream.

12.4.8 Scrambling

In systems where the structured spectrum resulting from a repetitive data signal might interfere with other signals, or with other components of the same signal, that data is scrambled by modulo-two addition of a predetermined pseudorandom sequence. Digitized silence is such a repetitive data signal and so both NICAM 728 and the MAC/packet data are scrambled in this way. Scrambling also assists some methods of data clock recovery.

12.5   DATA PACKET STRUCTURE

There have been numerous national and international discussions among broadcasters about the relative merits of fixed data formats and systems supporting packets of variable length. The result is that most systems have a packet-like structure but with fixed-length packets which typically start with address and control information and end with redundant bits to provide an error check. The main examples of variable length packets are in telesoftware, whether by radio or teletext, where the information is sent in blocks typically 200-1000 bytes long and in Datacast where the packet length is adjusted usually to fill but never to exceed the available capacity on a data line. The length and format of the packets depend on the application and some examples are now given.

12.5.1 LF radio-data

Figure 12.4a shows the LF radio-data packet of length 50 bits. At such a slow data rate a long packet would take a significant time to receive and process, even if it only carried a short message. The size was chosen to suit the expected message types and to be a submultiple of one minute in duration, to simplify its use in time-related activities. The blocks are phased so that one immediately precedes the change of minute and this carries a time and date message.

Although a fixed leading bit is provided to assist a decoder in synchronizing with the block structure, it is intended that decoders use the 13-bit check word for synchronization. In effect, the decoder tests all possible block boundaries and latches on to the one which consistently satisfies the redundancy check after every 50-bit block period. Because of the slow data rate this operation can be done by software.

12.5.2 RDS

The RDS format shown in Figure 12.4b is based on packets of only 26 bits, ten of which provide the redundancy check. The packet size was chosen after extensive field measurements of error patterns under adverse reception conditions, such as in a moving vehicle in mountainous terrain. In order to provide a larger message unit these are grouped into blocks of four.

The same implied synchronization is used as in LF radio-data but with four different ten-bit words added, bit-wise modulo-two, in sequence to the ten-bit check words. The decoder can lock on to this pattern and so achieve group and packet synchronization.

RDS was developed from a Swedish paging system and codes are provided to allow such a system to co-exist without confusing the decoder.

12.5.3 Teletext and Datacast

The length of the teletext packet is determined by the number of bits which can be signalled within the television active line period of $52\mu s$. When the display standard of teletext was decided at 40 characters per row of text there was a strong wish to encode information on a one row per line basis. Figure 4c shows the structure. Two bytes of 1010... clock run-in sequence were provided to give bit synchronization followed by an eight-bit framing code to give byte synchronization.

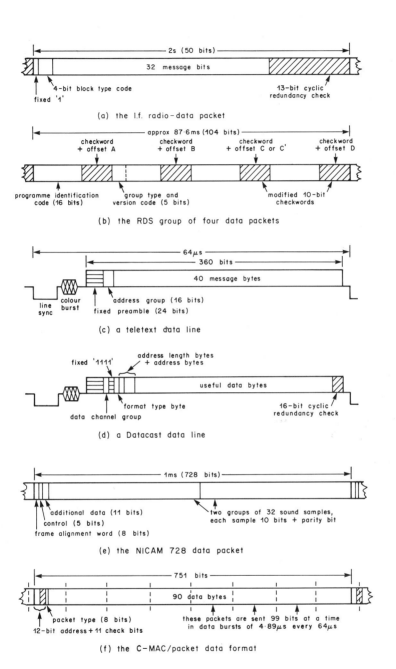

Fig.12.4 - Broadcast data packet formats.

Addressing was kept to a minimum by using only eight bits, three to indicate one of eight magazines and five to indicate one of 32 rows, only 24 of which were to be used. These eight address bits were encoded as two 8,4 Hamming coded bytes to give protection against errors. The boundaries between pages of a magazine were marked by page headers (row 0) which, exceptionally, used the next eight codes for further address and control instead of as character codes. So there are 45 bytes (360 bits) in a teletext data line, and in most lines 320 of these bits represent useful data.

Datacast uses the teletext data line format but it uses some of the eight-bit address codes which are ignored by a teletext decoder to provide four independent channel groups. The remaining 40 bytes then become available for redefinition, as shown in Figure 12.4d. The first byte specifies the following format in more detail, whether packets are repeated, how the continuity index is sent, and whether the packet is deliberately shortened. The next byte specifies the length of the packet address, which can be 0, 4, 8, 12, 16, 20 or 24 bits. After the address and control bytes come the useful data bytes followed by a 16-bit cyclic redundancy check. Between 28 and 36 bytes of useful data are available per line, depending on the format selected. Unlike teletext, every Datacast line can be checked and interpreted in isolation.

12.5.4 NICAM 728

The NICAM 728 data is gathered into 728-bit packets (frames) of 1ms duration as shown in Figure 12.4e. This fits well with the NIC operation which compands blocks of 1ms of sound (32 samples). The NICAM 728 packet contains two groups of 32 sound samples, corresponding to a stereo pair or 2ms of sound from one source, with each sample coded as ten bits plus a parity bit. The range code for each sound block is signalled as a three bit number, each bit being signalled by the parity of nine particular samples being odd or even. The sound accounts for 704 bits of the packet. Eight bits are used for a frame alignment word to give packet synchronization, and five bits are used for control functions which indicate how the sound channels are used or whether they are available for other data services. The remaining 11 bits per millisecond are, at present, available as an additional data channel. Although Figure 12.4e indicates that the 64 11-bit sound samples are sent in sequence this part of the packet is bit-interleaved prior to transmission.

12.5.5 MAC/packet

All members of the MAC/packet family use 751-bit packets as indicated in Figure 12.4f. The first 23 bits comprise a 23,12 Golay code which is unusual in being perfectly packed. Twelve message bits are protected by a further 11 check bits and there is a complete correspondence between the 2048 possible check syndromes and the $1 + 23 + 253 + 1771 = 2048$ possible patterns of no, one, two or three errors distributed among 23 bits. So this code can correct triple errors but, of course, it will falsely 'correct' four or more errors. This powerful code is used to send a twelve-bit packet address which, in the case of digital sound, is taken to be a ten-bit packet address associated with a two-bit continuity index to provide indication of packet loss or gain.

The next byte is a packet type indicator, whose function is well defined for sound signals where it allows control packets to be inserted into the series of sound packets. The remaining 90 bytes carry sound samples which, as with NICAM 728, are bit-interleaved.

In normal use the MAC/packet system will have ample spare data capacity, and packet addresses, available for other data services and the EBU is studying methods of using this capacity. One possible approach defines several possible error correcting codes to be used in the data field, including the use of the Golay code.

12.6 APPLICATIONS

Some of the systems described above were designed for specific applications. The LF radio-data system was primarily intended for the 'teleswitching' system for load management and tariff control in the electricity supply industry [11]. The service is very reliable and the frequency used allows reception within buildings even below ground level. The service also offers a source of time and date.

RDS is primarily intended to offer a programme identification service which, together with a list of alternative frequencies which can also be signalled by the system, allows a fixed or mobile receiver to search for a particular programme and to find the best available signal. It also provides the facility to send 64-character messages for display, using an eight-bit coded extended character set to meet the needs of most European countries. A time and date service is also provided, using Modified Julian Date and Coordinated Universal Time to be independent of time zone and calendar convention. As part of a European initiative a traffic message service, using densely-coded pre-defined messages (in seven languages) is being planned. It will use about 100 bit/s of the capacity.

Teletext is perhaps the most widespread and well-established of these data broadcasting services, with over thirty million receivers in use in over thirty countries. Datacast offers reliable, low cost transparent data channels for a variety of special uses, including the updating of databases and the distribution of specialist financial information to subscribers. It could also be used to provide information to control domestic equipment, such as a video cassette recorder.

NICAM 728 was designed to offer digital two-channel or stereo sound with television, but some broadcasters have already expressed an interest in using the system to carry data services.

The MAC/packet system offers great flexibility both as a television system and as a data carrier. It is too early to say how this flexibility will be used.

12.7 ACKNOWLEDGMENTS

The author wishes to thank the Director of Engineering of the British Broadcasting Corporation for permission to publish this contribution. Datacast is a Registered Trade Mark of the British Broadcasting Corporation.

12.8 REFERENCES

1   Wright, BBC Engineering Division Research Department Report 1988/10 Conditional Access Broadcasting: Datacare 2.

2   EBU, Brussels, October 1986, Tech.3258-E Specification of the systems of the MAC/packet family.

3   Wright, BBC Engineering Division Research Department Report 1984/19 L.F.RADIO-DATA: Specification of BBC phase-modulated transmissions on long-wave.

4   EBU, Brussels, March 1984, Tech.3244-E (includes two supplements) Specifications of the radio data system RDS for VHF/FM sound broadcasting.

5   Bower, August 1987, IEEE Trans. Consumer Electronics CE-33 Digital Two-channel Sound for Terrestrial Television.

6   Chambers, BBC Engineering Division Research Department Report 1985/15 Signalling in Parity: a Brief History.

7   BBC,IBA,BREMA, September 1976, Broadcast Teletext Specification.

8   Chambers, April 1987, EBU Review (Technical) No.222, pp80-89. BBC Datacast.

9   Kallaway and Mahadeva, BBC Engineering Division Research Department Report 1977/15 CEEFAX: Optimum transmitted pulse shape.

10 Shelswell et al, BBC Engineering Division Research Department Report 1986/7 VSB 2-PSK: A modulation system for digital sound with television.

11 Edwardson et al, 1982, Fourth International Conference on Metering, Apparatus and Tariffs for Electricity Supply, IEE Conf. Publ. No. 217 A Radio Teleswitching System for Load Management in UK.

Chapter 13

Information Systems

Peter Karry

13.1 SETTING THE SCENE

13.1.1 Introduction

It is the impact of the application of all the various technologies that makes Data Communications and Networking vitally important to our quality of life.

In the UK, Industry needs to take a firm grasp of the fact that services have become more important than manufacture to our productivity and profitability. Key to this is the flow of information.

Some flows of information have become common place and standard; the potential for others is bounded only by the imagination which people can employ. There is plenty of information held in databases, and the opportunity for using this information is stimulated by convergence on one hand, and by divergence on the other.

In this chapter we will explore some examples of how Industry is changing through the use of Competitive Advantage, and also how this is changing the environment in which we live and work.

On the one hand, the data available to people, accessing it via a network, has provided a new source of information by **looking at it in new ways.** On the other hand, the fact that information is available on a network encourages more people to **access it in new ways.**

These changes have invaded all segments of our world to such an extent that the subject is very large, and so only a subset of them can be explored in this section.

The section will investigate where information services **have come from,** what we have **today,** and **where this could lead.** As a conclusion, we can look at the issues that are going to concern us within this sphere of influence.

13.1.2 History

The telephone has become accepted as a way of life in business and at home. Not only have they become networked, so that you can dial someone in China as readily as your next door neighbour, but there is a huge variety of information services available to you from a variety of providers e.g.

- **Road Conditions**
- **Weather**
  - **Todays recipe**
  - **Horoscopes**
  - **Health Advice**

In recent years, networking has brought data as well as voice to most businesses, and the pressure on profit margins has led increasingly to a drive to gain competitive advantage.

The impact, and the trends, can be seen by looking at those market segments which have taken to using networking to help them in this drive. These particularly include:-

> **Travel/Transport**
> **Leisure**
> **Finance**
> **Health**
> **Retail**
> **Textiles**

The use of networks already ranges through a complete spectrum of services and applications from Inter-company to Intra-Company. There has been a rapid growth of organizations focussing on specialist areas as can be seen by ICL's creation of the INS Joint Venture with Geisco who have a Worldwide thrust into the EDI marketplace. Currently INS have 1100 users, and there already exists a worldwide EDI community of 5000 users.

Another range of services, more readily related to interactive applications, are those offered by VANS (Value-added network service) suppliers. These include reservation systems and the potential for global leisure games, such as the National Bingo Game, also run by INS.

13.1.3 The Phases

In order to appreciate the scale of the operation which can be affected by the benefits the technology can afford, the NHS has just made a major announcement that it is adopting an EDI strategy. The Health industry is huge in the UK with

- Manufacturers earning **£5Bn p.a.**
- Balance of payments increasing by **£800M p.a.**
- Research spend of **£500M p.a.**
- Pharmacies sell **£2Bn** of drugs and health care p.a. through 12000 retail outlets

The size of the NHS =
> **14** Regional Health Authorities
> **190** District Health Authorities
> **2000** Hospitals
> Spending **£300M p.a.**

You will see later that there are clear advantages being provided today by easier exchange of information, but the trends into the future are about better ways to use the available information.

In fact, the point which I made earlier is worthy of closer inspection.

The first phase in the growth of usage of Information Services is:-

- New ways of working.

Just because the information is readily accessible and exchangeable electronically.

- New ways of knowing.

Because the users begin to realize that they can use the information for additional purposes.

The third phase is:-

- New ways of thinking,

because the user then begins to realize that he can undertake additional tasks, either by adding to the information, or by involving his own customers.

Following that the cycle becomes repetitive, with additional -
New ways of working - being brought into the business cycle, and we start all over again.

13.2 INFORMATION SERVICES TODAY

We can now look at some of the examples of where the application of Information Services is having an impact. These have become so widespread that I have decided to take a few examples, and have broken these down into the major markets specified earlier.

13.2.1 Leisure

Here one of the more serious applications has been into a not-too-serious game of Bingo. The falling attendances at the Bingo Halls of some years ago plus the threat posed by the newspapers added to an urge to create a **National Bingo Game**. Some 850 Bingo Halls have access to an X25 Information Service provided by INS which has an inbuilt level of security and resilience, which now permits anyone buying a ticket in any of those halls to play in the same game as any other player at the other end of the UK. Not only can the winner earn huge prizes 364 days a year, but in addition the involved leisure companies have reported increased business benefit, and are even now considering running such a game twice a day.
Once the opportunity is there, no reason exists not to try and exploit it further.

13.2.2 Retail

13.2.2.1 Home Shopping In France, terminals have been provided to people's homes, initially so that the population could easily access:-

- **Directory Enquiries,** without the need to access an operator
- **Railway Timetables**
- **Chattines (Messageries)**
- **Astrological Predictions**

These quickly became further used for **Home Banking**, which has been successful because a population of users was created early.
But the next stage was a move into **Teleshopping** in a number of discrete areas of large value items such as:-

- Clothing
- Home Appliances
- Toys
- Furniture
- with guarantied 48 hour delivery

After that, there was no barrier against offering a full range of **Home Shopping** just by adding to the list of suppliers to this service and now, within a 48 hour delivery, you can also get:

Groceries, Drinks, Food, Dairy, Beauty, Wine and Video, products.

13.2.2.2 EDI   Electronic Data Interchange has now expanded from linking the supermarket to the initial wholesale supplier market area into additional communities of trading clusters. For example ICL's subsidiary INS now services:

> Brewing
> Clothing
> Tobacconists
> Newsagents
> DIY
> Electronics
> Home Shopping
> Publishing
> and White Goods, amongst others.

The concept is very simple; it is an exchange of documents electronically between remote computers of many manufacturers, at a time of dispatch which suits the sender and time of delivery which suits the recipient.

In fact, the time has come when <u>not</u> having an EDI facility means that companies lose competitive advantage, and many large organizations are demanding that their suppliers must use this method of communication.

13.2.2.3 Phone-In-Drive-Through   A variation to Home Shopping (or Tele Shopping) is to ensure that a shopping trip is made speedy.

Operations exist where you can phone in your order which is accepted by the operator. Then on arrival you enter your ID, your order and price are confirmed, you write a cheque, pick up the order and leave; all within 4 minutes.

13.2.3 Government

In both the spheres of Local Government and of Central Government, networked information is becoming a way of life. Not only have we seen the requirement for a Government Data Network, for all Government departments to use for aspects such as Electronic Mail, but

> - EDI is helping the simplification of International Trade   Procedures, and HM Customs are quoted as saying **"In truth,   we can't guarantee a satisfactory   service   non-electronically   through   these   ports now"**.

> - Local Government has accepted that the use of an   Information Service is a way to offer better, more   cost-effective, services to their customers - that is , you or I. Councils like Islington have turned their   Neighbourhood office into a point of sale, with instant   access to **pay rent, check benefits, check waiting lists**   for housing or repair.

13.2.4 Travel/Transport

The very nature of this industry suggests a dispersed community of users, with many options - either in the type of travel chosen or in the type of organization to be used. Lots of **airlines**, lots of **car hire** firms, **tour operators** etc.

13.2.4.1 London Transport   In order to cure two major concerns, queues and fraud, LT have moved into automated tube ticketing. It may not be apparent that these are networked, but they are.

The feedback of information allows for better planning, easier fare revision, and passing revenue between their collaborators like London Buses, British Rail and the Docklands Light Railway.

13.2.4.2 Hertz Another way an Information Service is going to help you and I, is that Hertz have created a Database of Information which allows them to give us a customized print, of what motorways and exits to use, where to turn, how long the trip should take. Obviously, with access to more Databases, they could offer even more information. More of that later.

13.2.4.3 Airline Systems Using reservation systems via networked terminals have now become an accepted way of life in Travel Agents.

This has happened because of several factors. These include the fact that the Airlines' distribution channels are widely distributed, and also that they are desperately seeking competitive advantage to maximize their seat occupancy.

American Airlines set up a booking system on which they were always listed first, although all major airlines schedules were available. That service expanded to include **Telemarketing,** providing **Marketing surveys** and **Telethon** pledges.

From there, they offered a system ('Easysolve') to give

- cheapest flights around the world
- weather in destinations (e.g. London)
- Free miles on an advantage card

Now the extent of this system is such that the Chairman of American Airlines has been quoted as **'Faced with the choice, I would rather sell the airline than the Information Service'**

As a comparison leading to the same convergence, Japan Airlines created a Reservation system for seat booking, but decided to re-sell the use of that system, so that alternative reservations can be made at the same time, i.e. for

- Worldwide Sports Events
- Plays
- Concerts

because they have taken the view that a total service is needed to **"buy Wimbledon tickets for customers who are flying to London".**

Then with access to weather forecasts on the same network, the customer can decide where he wants to go to see the kind of leisure activity he likes best.

13.2.5 Financial Systems

In this segment of the marketplace, changes have already occurred with a direct impact in everyone's life.

Because of networked Information Services, you now act as a Bank Clerk or a petrol station cashier every week, in addition to your own job.

Everyone in the UK knows of the day called **'The Big Bang'**. This revolution was only able to happen with an explosion in the Information Systems available to be used by the Stock Exchange and associated communities.

13.2.5.1 Building Societies For example, Building Societies have expanded their sphere of influence to encompass not only Insurance companies, but also Estate Agencies, Conveyancing, as well as Stocks and Shares dealing. They are finding ways to compete with the Banks.

13.2.5.2 Insurance Companies In the same manner, Insurance Companies have taken to using EDI systems (such as the one INS offer), so that Agents can easily access more lines of business than their traditional ones. For example, Motor

Insurance agents not only get easy access to quotes from different **Motor Insurance** companies (allowing them to offer the lowest quote for a stated car/owner combination), but also to be able to offer life and household insurance as well. This of course gives the Insurance companies much information about how successful they have been. In addition, they can of course offer instantaneous Rating amendments.

13.2.6 Pharmaceutical Industry

One of the notable drives which occurred early in this field, was created by a Drugs and Health products distribution company called McKesson.

In the mid-70's, this unit was losing money. The business choices were to

- sell it
- fold it
- enhance it

The steps this organization took were

- to build internal systems
- offer these systems externally, by providing an Information Service
- to target a strategic thrust at their customers, small   chemists
- gave them free terminals, with a guarantee that 99% of all   items in all orders would be filled in 24 hours.
- gaining an insight into the data that customers were   sending them.
- selling the Information back to them
- selling the data onwards
- create a link to their own suppliers;
  and on we go.

13.3   MOVING INTO THE FUTURE

Several of the activities which are founded on a firm base of providing an Information Service today, indicate the route along which they may develop in the future. When you can spot the trends that are happening in one arena, you gain an insight into what can happen in other circumstances.

13.3.1 Local Government

County Councils :

We have already seen that the London Borough of Islington has changed its Neighbourhood office, and provides access to various type of networked Information.

Having moved on from providing some information to their community, any local council could move other services onto the available information, such as

- **Meals on wheels**
- **Care for elderly**
- **Refuse collection**

Then a potential step could be further contracting out of the services the council currently provides, to third parties. It would be a relatively easy step to ensure that the subcontractors linked to the community via a network. A possible further step could be that any member of the community could have a choice in which services they want to use - and only pay a charge relative to the services used.

Libraries :

It is already possible, for example, on an ICL Viewdata system at Berkshire, for people to reserve books from the Library by using a terminal. This is a similar system to reserving a flight.

This has been extended so that

Debenhams
Local Accountants
Local Solicitors

can all advertise their services, and in some cases, a reply paid enquiry is generated by the system.
A follow on could be to make information available at the library:

- where **road works** are happening
- **useful telephone** numbers for service providers (e.g. electronic Thompsons/Yellow Pages)

A further step could be to offer access to other Libraries, so that there could be a wider choice of books readily available. The **consumers use** and **level of interest** in authors, topics, or media, could then be sold back to publishers.
Eventually, books could go onto Video form, access provided to your home and you could read any book in the comfort of your armchair.
As a generality, you can see that boundaries are beginning to fall across Local Authority territories, and this could extend to the EEC very readily.

13.3.2 Central Government

Today, one of the largest networks is run by the Inland Revenue, running the National Tracing System. This can be accessed by 650 tax offices in the UK, and

- tracks down tax avoiders
- identifies people as they move
- permits enquiries on people who have written in without a reference

But, increasingly, as people have additional sources of income, or outgoings, from private pensions, into health care plan; shares; this creates a number of tax existences.
So the system needs to link into these other organizations and to allow you and I to owe tax in one place and pay it in another.
Submitting tax returns probably does not appeal to most people, so an alternative approach could be just to specify the various places where one has a tax existence and let a networked Information Service gather the detail.

13.3.3 Fashion

There are systems available today which give a interactive access to **designing clothes**, with a visual representation. Access to this could be offered to the marketeers as well as the designers, so that the international mix can be taken into account. This can be further extended to other similar design areas, **furniture, car design** and **footwear**.
In the future, all this could be screened to the desk top, so that buyers and suppliers could view this in separate offices and communicate changes verbally as well as graphically.

13.3.4 The Post Office

The Post Office already provides links from their major offices to suppliers of the services they offer e.g.

- **Road Tax**
- **GIRO Bank**
- **DHSS**
- **TV Licence**

and **25 million people** visit a Post Office every week.

Counter Automation is to take the Post Office forward, with a terminal on every counter display station to give instant access, and reduce counter queue delay. This is of interest to many other organizations:

- Insurance Companies
- Building Societies
- Rail Companies
- Bus Companies

so that the Post Office could act just like any other Retail outlet, and offer a customer a wider range of services.

13.4. THE FUTURE FOR INFORMATION SERVICES

More properly, the title should read "Is there any future for us without Information Services" and the answer would of course be "no". The extent to which we are already dependent on Information Services, governing both our business and our private lives, shows that this dependence is addictive. Without the information, we will not be able to match the increasing pressure to produce more productivity in our work and a better quality of life in our leisure. This section will investigate some of the pointers which suggest how these pressures can be eased.

13.4.1 Travel

One of the areas of greatest congestion in the UK today is that of wheeled transport, and minds are being increasingly turned to addressing this issue.

One approach is to offer a system such as Autoguide, which is being piloted. This could offer a two-way dialogue, providing both a central computer and the drivers with an **update of the traffic flows**, which could be applied to a logged route inside the vehicle.

Such a system could interact with **flight or shipping** information for vehicles on their way abroad.

Equally, there could be links to the **police, motorway** control, **ambulance** and **fire** services, with input from meteorological offices for weather predictions.

Could this lead to semi-automated traffic flows around the UK ?

13.4.2 Health

We are all aware of the proposed pressure on Doctor's surgeries and practices.

Activities involving consultants, hospital records and client records could all be readily accessible regardless of where a consultation is to take place, with the G.P., the records, any X-Rays, and specialist consultant, all being located in separate locations.

With the advent of remote diagnosis, even the patient could be in another location, and the doctor's bedside manner may need to turn to a good television manner.

13.4.3 Cashless Society

The moves which have already been taking place with plastic cards (building societies such as Link and Matrix collaborating) and the general convergence of the financial community, is pointing the way to an increasing use of EFTPOS.

The technology, the drive of the retailers towards becoming financial institutions, and EFTPOS, are showing that a direct debit from ones personal account, could well become a reality.

13.4.4 Workforce Mobility

Many of the technologies you have learnt of in this series, will enable information to be distributed anywhere and at any time. Beaming information to one's home, to urban or rural areas, or indeed to anywhere in Europe, for example, is going to be easy using

- **ISDN**
- **Satellite Services**
- **Microwave**
- **Cellular**

and companies will be able to send

- information to their **shareholders**
- corporate communication to the **workforce** at their desk
- instantaneous **price** changes
- software to your **home P.C.**
- **promotional** videos to their retailers

Already the financial marketplace is taking advantage of holding breakfast video conferences, and you can see the advantage of communicating between Stock Exchanges around the world (who are at different time zones) less mindful of the current days operating hours.

13.4.5 Energy Conservation

Companies continue to invest in creating new buildings, and in the future it will be standard for the controls within these buildings to be interconnected, so that one central system can be computerized with sophisticated

- security
- climatic control
- energy management
- lighting controls
- lift usage

13.5. SUMMARY

The capabilities offered by technology in the future seem only to be bounded by the imagination of the users.

Today we are looking at

- an increasing drive towards **privatization** by the   government
- a greater demand for **value for money** by the consumers

- more people retired than at work
- dropping of **national boundaries**

The advent of

- moving into 1992 **Europe**
- growing **communities of interest** wanting to exchange   information electronically
- businesses able to **interfunction** across Zonal boundaries,   with scarce skills deployed in the appropriate places
- **branding** of services being key to the way businesses   expand into large conglomerates

shows that the way Information Services are provided is going to be one of the keys to business success in the future.

Index

adaptive equalizer, 46, 146
alternate mark inversion (AMI), 39, 68
amplitude modulation, 41
applications level (layer), 17, 56
ARQ, 64. 144, 145, 150
asynchronous, 38, 93, 124
Autofahrer Rundfunk Information (ARI), 157

BASICODE, 155
basic rate access, 98, 99, 112
B channel, 98, 103, 112
bearer service, 109
biphase, 162
bus, 21

cable TV, 19
Cambridge ring, 119
CCITT, 6, 59, 82, 128
CCITT No.7 signalling system, 108
Ceefax, 20
Cellnet, 138
cellular mobile radio, 95, 138, 177
chaining, 77
coaxial cables, 20
convolution code, 67, 141
CSMA/CD, 59, 94, 116, 117
cyclic redundancy check code, 48, 66

Dass 2, 112
Datacast, 20, 152, 161, 162, 164
data encryption standard (DES), 77
D channel, 98, 103, 112
differential phase-shift keying (DPSK), 41, 43
DQDB, 126
duobinary code, 70, 163

echo canceller, 34, 47, 52
echoes, 28
ECMA, 59
electronic code book (ECB), 77
electronic data interchange (EDI), 172
electronic funds transfer (EFT), 14, 177
encryption, 74, 77
equalization, 45, 92
error control, 23
error correction, 48, 64

error detection, 64
Ethernet, 21, 116

facsimile, 96
fading, 140
fast fax, 113
featurephones, 114
fibre distributed data interface (FDDI), 121
fibre optics - see optical fibres
file transfer access and management (FTAM), 17
forward error correction, 64, 141, 150
flexible access systems (FAS), 113
frequency division multiplex, 1,47 155
frequency modulation, 39
frequency shift keying (FSK), 39, 145, 157, 162
full duplex, 8

gateway, 136
Gray coding, 43
Groupe Speciale Mobile (GSM), 139, 149

Hagelbarger code, 67
Hamming code, 65, 166
HDB3 code, 74
High-level data link control (HDLC), 11, 94, 95
Hobbyscope, 155
HSLANs, 116, 121
Huffman coding, 63
hybrid ring control, 125

ideal channel, 29
IEEE, 59
IEEE 802 series, 96
IEEE 802.3, 59
IEEE 802.6, 126
impairments, 139
information services, 176
information transfer, 136